Questions for Life
Powerful Strategies
to Guide Critical Thinking

Also by Stephen G. Barkley

Quality Teaching in a Culture of Coaching

WOW: Adding Pizzazz to Teaching and Learning

Tapping Student Effort: Increasing Student Achievement

Questions for Life
Powerful Strategies
to Guide Critical Thinking

Stephen G. Barkley

with Terri Bianco

a special introduction by Joseph K. Hasenstab

PERFORMANCE
LEARNING SYSTEMS.

Performance Learning Systems, Inc.®
Publications Division

© 2009 Performance Learning Systems, Inc.
All Rights Reserved.
Printed in the United States of America
10 9 8 7 6 5 4 3 2 1

PLS® Products
72 Lone Oak Drive
Cadiz, KY 42211
800-506-9996
Fax 270-522-2014
http://www.plsweb.com/QFL

Library of Congress Cataloging-to Publication Data

Barkley, Stephen G. (Stephen George), 1950-
Questions for life: powerful strategies to guide critical thinking /
    by Stephen G. Barkley, with Terri Bianco;
    a special introduction by Joseph K. Hasenstab.
p. cm.
    Includes bibliographical references and index.
    ISBN-13: 978-1-892334-26-8 (pbk. : alk. paper)
    ISBN-10: 1-892334-26-7 (pbk. : alk. paper)
1. Critical thinking. I. Bianco, Terri. II. Title.
LB1590.3.B365 2009
370.15'2–dc22

                              2009024299

Cover and Internal Design: Sharon Bieganski-Negron,
    Blonde Renditions Creative Studio
Index: Brackney Indexing Service
Adobe Fonts: ITC Cheltenham and Cosmos

This book may be ordered from Performance Learning Systems®
72 Lone Oak Drive, Cadiz, KY 42211, 800-506-9996.
Quantity discounts availablve for bulk purchases, sales, promotions,
premiums, fund-raising, and educational needs.

This is a Worthy Shorts BackOffice Print-on-Demand Edition
ISBN: 978-1-935340-92-8   PLS101P

Produced and distributed for Performance Learning Systems
by Worthy Shorts BackOffice Publisher Services

For information please visit:
www.worthyshorts.com/performance/bookshop.php

Printed in the U.S.A.

Dedication

*It is my special privilege to dedicate this book
to Joseph K. Hasenstab, the founder of
Performance Learning Systems, Inc.*

*Joe has been my employer, teacher, colleague, mentor,
and friend since 1976. At that time, having already received my
undergraduate and graduate degrees in education, I enrolled in an
intriguing graduate-level education course for teachers called* Project
TEACH. *This course, designed by Joe, was my first experience with
a concrete set of skills I could immediately use in my classroom.
More importantly, it identified teachers as professionals who, with
knowledge and practice of specific skills, could readily achieve
excellence in teaching. My introduction to that course and to
Performance Learning Systems ultimately led to my decision to
partner with Joe in implementing his dream to provide students
with the best-trained teachers in the world.*

*Questions for Life® is perhaps Joe's most brilliant design, showing
how a complex proficiency can be presented in an understandable,
usable, and trainable format for teachers and students alike. I am
delighted that Joe has penned the Introduction to this book.*

*Thank you, Joe, for all you have done for me,
for teachers, for students, and for all who have benefited
from your passion for quality education.*

Contents

Acknowledgments

It takes a team to write a book. *Questions for Life: Powerful Strategies to Guide Critical Thinking* is no exception.

From inception to printing, writing a book requires research, creativity, new ideas, old ideas, input from a variety of sources, synthesizing, collaborating, fine-tuning and much writing, editing, and producing.

I would like to first thank and acknowledge Dr. Ronald L. Partin. He is the author of a well-received book that also took a team to build, *Classroom Teachers' Survival Guide: Practical Strategies, Management Techniques, and Reproducibles for New and Experienced Teachers.* Ron provided the research and guidance that kept our writing team accurate and accountable.

Terri Bianco, consultant, writer, and head of TBEnterprises, lent voice to my thoughts, collaborated on concepts, and made written sense out of ideas, experiences, and insights I have gathered as I travel through the world of education.

The following educators contributed ideas, classroom examples, lesson plans, and helpful reviews of our efforts. They did so out of their dedication to learning and their passion for Questions for Life.

Barbara DeVena, Galesburg, IL
Carolyn Flickinger, Wilkes-Barre, PA
Judi Lalli, Philadelphia, PA
Angelo Rivera, Elk Grove Village, IL
Betsy Varis, West Frankfort, IL
Dana Simpson-West, Fenton, MO
John and Chris Yeates, Richton Park, IL
Phyllis Younkins, Keedysville, MD
A special thanks to Barb DeVena, Carolyn Flickinger, and Dana Simpson-West for wonderful lesson plans that capture how Questions for Life plays out in the classroom.

A book would not be a book without the structure needed to make it work. For this I thank the team of Barbara Brown of Phil Brown Fine Arts for her stellar production-management abilities; Sharon Bieganski-Negron of Blonde Renditions Creative Studio for quality graphic design; Joanna Robinson for keeping the punctuation and syntax accurate and flowing; Michael Brackney of Brackney Indexing Service for the comprehensive index; and various members of the Performance Learning Systems staff who graciously provided help: Don Jacobs, Kathy Schmied, Carla Minks, Chris Juhasz, Beth Eck, Nancy Seay, and Jackie Futrell.

Last, but certainly not least, I would like to thank Joseph K. Hasenstab, whose steadfast adherence to sound educational principles has steered me in my career for several decades. Joe has a mind in which ideas bubble up, regroup to percolate some more, and come forth again, each time in ways that are timeless and profound. Our hope in writing this book is that Questions for Life, which is Joe's creation, will make a positive and substantial difference in the lives of all who read it.

Introduction
by Joseph K. Hasenstab

As a kid, I suffered from dyslexia. No one talked about it back then, I didn't even know I had it. I just knew that it was tough getting through school and I had to work hard to read and do my lessons.

I noticed that some teachers who worked with me got through to me, inspired me, and helped me learn. Others did not. We couldn't connect and I wondered why.

The dyslexia somehow cured itself, and I made it successfully through school and on to college. I ended up becoming a teacher myself. I taught for ten years in two school districts. There again, I noticed that some teachers seemed to succeed with students and enjoy teaching, while others were frustrated, unable somehow to get through to their students on any consistent basis.

Again, I wondered why.

I began to interview and study the teachers whose skills and performance patterns produced results—the ones people considered their "best" teachers. These were the educators whose verbal and nonverbal skills, strategies, and decision making shone; they seemed to have more tools in their tool kits. They could read their students and anticipate their next moves.

I left teaching and formed a company in New Jersey whose sole purpose was to develop excellent teachers. I founded Performance Learning Systems, Inc. (PLS) in 1973, and we began by identifying, cataloging, and training 180 skills and performance patterns that constituted successful teaching. In the end I made two great decisions: looking at the world of teaching through the eyes of the teachers and hiring "best" teachers to serve as our instructors.

For over 35 years I served as president of PLS, expanding its educational services, techniques, and resources to a national—and now international—level. At 55 I retired, satisfied with a job well done and ready to let the company continue its growth with a new generation of teachers and students.

PLS operates in concert with universities and state teacher organizations that train classroom teachers through multiple 45-hour graduate-level courses, both live and online. All courses yield measurable learning. The company offers professional development, educational materials, and consultation with educators at all levels. PLS has been called the "West Point" of training for teachers. All of this means we know something about education.

The PLS vision to provide children with the best-trained teachers in the world drives the company's mission to improve the art of teaching. We do that through techniques and strategies that ensure effective teaching, which in turn leads to successful student learning. In the process of developing these approaches to teaching, I created Questions for Life. I think it's my best work. And the reason it's my best work is that it applies to learning and teaching in all aspects of education and, more importantly, in all aspects of living. That's why we called it Questions for Life.

Architects of Information

Periodically during my career—and now on the golf course—I pose a hypothetical question to educators, businesspeople, parents, students, or whoever shows an interest in education. The question I pose is this: If every student memorized every textbook provided in school, would that prepare him or her to be successful in life? The unanimous answer is no. Why isn't the answer a thundering yes?

The no comes from the knowledge that content in textbooks does not necessarily transfer to the skills and clarity of thought students need to navigate successfully through life. What they need is a sound set of skills and the ability to think critically so they can question, analyze, predict, create, and act effectively.

To borrow a term from Web professionals, students need to become "architects of information." They need to learn to build on knowledge that is relevant to them and that provides them with a solid foundation on which to base the many decisions they will have to make in response to the vicissitudes of life.

The desire of humans to learn is innate; learning is a survival mechanism of the human brain. Our brains do not come replete with knowledge as do the brains of creatures who function instinctively, knowing, for example, how to camouflage themselves as jungle plants or head blindly toward their home in the sea as soon as they are born. We have to learn, and our brains are hardwired to do that.

Our early ancestors were hunters and gatherers who had to develop strategies, use thought processes, and develop language to catch game for food and clothing. Spears, arrows, and clubs were the weapons they used to achieve their goals, which were driven by basic needs. Our predecessors learned to distinguish the habits of the different animals and the hazardous or beneficial impacts of the various plants in their environments. They made these distinctions by recognizing patterns. Observing, listening, smelling, touching, and tasting afforded them the ability to appraise, develop preferences, and see connections.

In short, early human beings had to learn how to think clearly, correctly, and strategically in order to survive. They had to practice and become clever at it. Fast-forward to now, and we see that our species has developed a vastly larger vocabulary, a sensitive emotional system, and the growth of the frontal cortex, where highly complex reflection occurs. Yet we continue to need to think clearly, correctly, and strategically in order to thrive. One purpose of school lies in building happy, healthy, successful adults who contribute to our planet, our society, and to the country's tax base.

Unlike other creatures, mankind, in this highly complex and ever-changing world, needs tools to guide him. That is why we created Questions for Life.

Questions for Life: A Tool for Thinking

Questions for Life is a tool that provides a way to focus on critical thinking when addressing core subjects, textbook content, and real-life situations. Questions for Life works the way the brain works. It is relevant and meaningful to all learners, whether they are students, educators, or those working in nonacademic environments. The structure of Questions for Life provides a road map for navigating the thinking process purposefully and successfully. It offers opportunities to strategize using questioning processes designed to elicit critical thinking.

The Questions for Life model is attuned to brain development and backed by significant research that makes it substantially more valuable than any new model or "gimmick" teachers often come across. It is much more powerful than that. First and foremost it is a tool for the educator, and secondly, it is a tool for students.

According to a report titled *Tough Choices or Tough Times* by the National Center on Education and the Economy, "the problem is not with our educators.[1] It is the system within which they work." It is a system that requires educators to postpone their own reflection, thinking, and strategic planning to make time to muddle through mandates and meet state standards. It is a system that offers few opportunities for teachers or students to stop and think as they move ahead into a future that will be so altered from today's experience as to be almost unrecognizable. To respond effectively to these new circumstances, the system must be changed to allow teachers to acquire, embody, and impart the skills and thinking processes their students need to know.

Teachers will need to shift how and what they teach. There can be no change in how students learn if there is no corresponding shift in how teachers teach. Most studies of skills people use in the workplace speak to the need for students to be taught to think, decide, and act. Too often teachers do the thinking, deciding, and acting for their students. A significant shift takes place when teachers share the thinking processes they use with students, allowing students to do the thinking, problem solving, and decision making. Questions for Life is a tool for creating that change.

And here I want to express my appreciation for and pride in the instructors who teach Questions for Life, some of whom have developed teaching examples found in the Appendix of this book. Their modeling and that of hundreds of other instructors have inspired thousands of teachers to improve their questioning practices. Learning to use reflexive questioning processes takes a huge investment in effort, yet the rewards are terrific. Teachers see the difference in their students' eyes as they grasp their own thinking process and the power it holds.

The Need for Change

There is no question that there is and has been a dire need for education to change. I know that and Steve Barkley, the author of this book, knows that. Steve was the first trainer and first employee at Performance Learning Systems. Now our Executive Vice President, Steve is a published author, brilliant trainer, colleague, and friend. As I did before him, Steve crisscrosses the country every week speaking to educators and championing the cause of improving education. We are both frustrated that change in education has not been more rapid. We have known for years there is a serious gap between how quickly students need to acquire skills to help them function in life successfully and how slowly and sluggishly the pace of the current educational process is going.

Meanwhile, change is coming—perhaps a tsunami of change. Transformations in demographics, economics, technology, and the workforce have created new conditions that will powerfully alter how we deliver and even frame education.

To be sure, there are promising pockets of innovation already opening up in education all over the country—some are highlighted in this book, such as charter schools, privately owned schools, grant-funded schools, and twenty-first-century schools. Many of these are trying various programs and approaches to improve learning, to prepare students for college, to meet educational standards, and to enable students to be competitive in the global economy.

While these attempts and their varying degrees of success are admirable, would it not be more logical to provide learning tools that shift the focus from "getting" students to learn to creating an environment where they will want—and be able—to learn?

Change is often resisted and feared, but it needn't be. The kinds of long overdue changes coming to education promise to unleash educators' abilities to be creative and to work with real-world applications, so students can become engaged and responsible for their learning as they see the direct impact it has on their lives.

At some critical point in the not too distant future there may well be some very dynamic and innovative changes in our education system. Perhaps one of the many new, privately funded charter schools will come across a formula that improves learning for all. Maybe it will be found that we do not need only one standard of education. In view of the diversity in our world and considering the multiple avenues of information available to us, including our newly acquired abilities to transcend cultures and language, maybe we can finally admit we have outgrown that one-size-fits-all standard as surely as we have outgrown buggy whips.

Meanwhile we can't wait any longer for all this to get sorted out. Regardless of changes in schools, what kids need to learn is how to think. And from thinking comes the ability to make crucial decisions and good choices that will lead to living and prospering in any environment.

My Passion

Learning requires passion. It requires the freedom to be curious and to discover a "fire in the belly" about something that has significance and meaning for the learner. When I attended what is now Truman State University in Missouri, my favorite professor held court after class at the Bulldog Café, discussing with willing students anything they wanted to discuss with him. Somehow over many cups of coffee, this valued professor sparked an interest for me in Clarence Darrow, the great "attorney of the damned." Darrow had been retained to defend the teenage thrill-killers Nathan Leopold and Richard Loeb, who murdered 14-year-old Bobby Franks. Later Darrow was called in to defend John T. Scopes, who violated the law by teaching evolution in his classroom. In the famous "monkey trial" that ensued, Darrow successfully opposed the lawyer, statesman, orator, and later presidential nominee William Jennings Bryan.

My professor sent me to the library to study the transcripts of these and others of Darrow's trials. I sat in the stacks, reading and studying, taking no tests and receiving no credit or grades—the subject had simply become my fire in the belly. I was in the zone. I was learning. I was thinking.

Darrow's questioning skills fascinated me. I studied his rhetoric and questioning processes to figure out what exactly made them so strategic and persuasive. Whether I agreed with him or not did not matter; I was intrigued by his skill at asking questions that led to the conclusions he drew in his brilliant summations. Obviously, these types of questioning skills had a tremendous influence on me. They remained with me and, along with other specifically identified teaching techniques, were a big part of the inspiration behind Performance Learning Systems.

The Questions for Life Model

We are bringing the Questions for Life model to a larger audience at this time because the need for change in education is so huge. Designed to elicit and generate high-level thinking, Questions for Life provides the scaffolding on which a person can build purposeful conversation and communication, whether in the classroom or around the globe. It opens the door to successful negotiation and provides a way for creative thoughts to develop and evolve into action. It allows us to be architects of information.

We all need to tackle enormous economic, social, environmental, technological, and cultural challenges—mighty changes are already upon us, and more are on the way. Rather than wait for educational reform, we offer a process *now* that teaches how to think about and manage whatever changes may come along.

Will a powerful questioning strategy alter the framework of education? Is it going to revolutionize current curriculum into one that teaches real-life skills, such as how to problem solve and how to create? Will it find ways to understand the value of going to college or where to invest money? Or how to communicate? How to be free, successful, and responsible?

Well, it's a start and a tool to get there—a tool that can help us think within the box well enough to find a way to get out of it and move into the larger world, just ahead of the tsunami.

Chapter 1
Ready or Not,
Here Comes Change!

The Illusion of Change

Every educator knows that technology and the speed of its information delivery systems far surpass the pace of chalk moving across a blackboard. The world is speeding up, expanding outward while also seeming to get smaller. Everywhere we turn, we hear the demand that education change in order to keep up. A serious problem arises when educators and students, swept up in the culture of busyness that permeates most schools, labor under the illusion that change *is* occurring, that they *are* keeping up.

Many factors help to create this illusion. It stems from the steady stream of students moving through schools and from the clamor of constantly clanging bells and beeping buzzers. There are always new mandates, new standards. Veteran educators can claim they've heard the heralding of change in education most of their adult lives, but when trying to envision the future, they are often blinded by the present. Swiftly passing years within the school system create an *illusion* of change in an environment where there is little time or encouragement to step back and reflect upon *real* change.

Meanwhile, with every ring of the bell and beep of the buzzer, with every graduation and matriculation, the nonacademic world is changing. Things move fast in this outside world, far faster than within the confines of institutions such as schools, despite the illusion of change that often prevails there. These changes in the outside world are not abstractions, and they are not challenges students can deal with *after* graduation. Nor are they changes educators can ignore because they seem to involve only young people. To think so would be myopic. These forces have a direct and immediate impact on what takes place in the classroom—and where they do not now, they soon will. Consider just a few changes that have recently had an impact on our schools: privatization, charter schools, teachers' pay structures, political reforms, economic trends, infrastructure concerns, and environmental requirements.

The Reality of Change

These big changes come from the realm of continuously developing trends in demographics, global economics, generational differences, a retiring workforce, ever-evolving technology, energy consumption, environmental issues, and a constant blend of language and cultures.

Asia has emerged as an enormous player in the international marketplace. The level of education in this part of the world exceeds our own, particularly in the areas of math and science. The workers of India, China, the Philippines, and other up-and-coming countries enjoy increased job security and employment in fields that Americans cannot or will not work in. In this country a huge retirement wave of 77 million professionals will create an employment vacuum, and there will be a shortage of workers to fill it.

With the rise of energy costs and the increase in telecommuting, we are now looking at very different ways of doing things. Why do we have to leave home to go to work? Or for that matter, why do students have to go to school to learn? According to Clayton Christensen, Curtis Johnson, and Michael Horn, the authors of *Disrupting Class: How Disruptive Innovation Will Change the Way the World Learns,*[1] nearly half of students' classes will be taken online by 2019. As technology becomes more and more portable, the growing web of connectivity will expand the classroom—and the workplace—far and wide.

In his influential book *The Black Swan: The Impact of the Highly Improbable*[2] Nassim Taleb describes the phenomenon of unpredictable events that come along to change the course of history. The book takes its name from the black swans of Australia: before the first European explorers arrived there in the seventeenth century, Europeans had never seen black swans. In their experience, empirical knowledge pointed to the assumption that all swans were white. When the explorers saw black swans, therefore, a whole new perspective opened up.

Other examples of "black swans" are the attacks of 9/11 and the invention of the Internet. Before these events occurred, no one could have predicted them; after they occurred, the world was a different place. Taleb believes that the existence of "black swans" underscores how fragile our knowledge really is.

Some of the changes coming to education may be predictable. We may speculate that "green" buildings will replace older, environmentally inefficient facilities. Employers—possibly including school districts—may be fined for not going green (or rewarded for efforts to do so). Being entrepreneurial and self-starting will be essential in the environment of telecommuting. The trend of Generation Y already leans toward working independently; Gen Ys do not see themselves as working "for" someone else. In like fashion, they may not see studying "for" the teacher as relevant either. Why not be entrepreneurial about what they learn and when they learn it?

Global economics, advanced technology, the Internet, social networking, volatile worldwide politics, a planet urgently in need of replenishing and preservation, and other changing aspects of this fast-paced world—including even second lives with avatars—suggest that a completely different focus for education is urgently needed.

And while the world may change before our eyes, the eyes of students will still look to educators for guidance, wisdom, and hope for the future. Those who express an urgent need for change in education, however, stress that students going through the classrooms of America today will not possess the skills, behaviors, or aptitudes necessary to successfully compete in tomorrow's labor force. They may find themselves with low wages, unsatisfactory employment, or an inferior standard of living compared to their counterparts in other parts of the world.

Without a college education, their prospects get worse. Those who opt not to go to college may be faced with a larger burden because of the way job outsourcing is leading to the demise of our manufacturing industry and its related fields. One in three high school students drops out of school every year, often from boredom or in protest against an education that does not serve real needs.

How did this happen? Books, theories, studies, and reports abound about the changing workforce and the skills it requires, yet we have an educational system that has been slow to respond. Laden with layers of standards and a focus on tried-and-true core subject matter, education, for the most part, has been left behind, becoming more and more irrelevant in the changing world. People in today's workforce need skills that enable them to be mentally nimble, innovative, and creative.

More importantly, education has not included in curriculum in any uniform or focused way skills of critical thinking that teach students how to solve complex, multidisciplinary problems. Crucial skills of creativity, entrepreneurial thinking, communication, collaboration, innovation, and civic responsibility have been mostly ignored.

To be sure, the core subjects that have been taught in schools for generations will continue to be necessary and desirable in education. The Partnership for 21st Century Skills, an organization consisting of both public and private institutions, was formed in 2002 to create a successful model of learning with a focus on identifying twenty-first-century skills and incorporating them into education. When reporting on the achievement gap between the lowest- and highest-performing students, the Partnership stated:

> People with only basic competencies are the most likely to flounder in the rising high-skill, high-wage service economy. To prepare students to be competitive, the nation needs "NCLB plus" agenda [No Child Left Behind] that infuses 21st century skills into core academic subjects. This is not an either-or agenda. Students can master 21st century skills while they learn reading, mathematics, science, writing, and other school subjects.[3]

Abundance, Asia, and Automation

Daniel H. Pink's *A Whole New Mind: Why Right-Brainers Will Rule the Future*[4] offers an alarming, yet lighthearted encapsulation of trends that are transforming the world in ways comparable to such dramatic shifts as moving from the Agricultural Age to the Industrial Age, and from the Industrial Age to the Information or Knowledge Age. He identifies three major forces that are causing a paradigm shift in the world: Abundance, Asia, and Automation.

Abundance

As a premise, Pink makes the point that skills and types of thinking used in the Knowledge Age, such as computing, linear thinking, logic, and analysis, are left-brained functions. (He refers to these as *left-directed,* or *L-directed, thinking.*) These skills and types of thinking have brought about technological breakthroughs and allowed us to create fast-speed services, global connections, and multiple products that give us the abundance we now enjoy.

But the abundance underscores Pink's point. We are, in fact, drowning in material goods and services that are becoming more and more available at lower and lower costs. Most essentials today cost less than they did in our parents' day simply because there are so many of them. Such proliferation engenders indifference: services and products have begun to lose significance to the consumer. We are now looking for products that are special—designer-based, aesthetic, and meaningful. These products must be created, and the creative process stems from right-directed thinking.

Asia

Pink shows how routine, "L-directed" white collar jobs, such as those in computer programming, financial services, radiology, news reporting, legal services, and similar linear and functional processes, are now being outsourced to India, China, the Philippines, Russia, and other countries where college graduates are earning a fraction of what Americans earned for doing the same work.

Left-brained jobs, in short, are going overseas, leaving Americans to find employment requiring more right-brained thinking that cannot be exported or duplicated by a computer. The new products and services derived from right-brained thinking tend to add significance to the abundance that surrounds us.

Automation

Pink points out that more and more functions formerly performed by humans can now be accomplished through automation and technology. Even software, he notes, can be designed by computers.

This situation again eliminates a need for entry-level workers and creates a need for workers who are more creative, collaborative, and innovative. In summary, Pink believes we are now moving out of the Knowledge Age to the Age of Conceptualization, in which these skills and more creative ways of thinking will be paramount.

Pink is not alone in urging the development of different skills for a different world. Eighty percent of American voters believe skills students need in order to be prepared for jobs in the future are vastly different from what they needed 20 years ago. Eighty-eight percent of voters believe schools should play a vital role in teaching these twenty-first-century skills.

Skills, Skills, and More Skills

To be fair, education today *does* prepare students for many types of careers, and it also prepares them to be better citizens and more successful human beings, regardless of workplace competition. Many educators are aware of changing trends and demographics, and they understand the impact technology has had on the world and the workplace. Yet few teachers have much direct control over how they will respond to these changes by better preparing students for successful future employment. Rather, educators spend their time struggling to prepare students for standardized tests, having insufficient opportunity to focus on their students' future careers and lives.

The word *skill* is defined in *Webster's New World College Dictionary* as "a great ability or proficiency; expertness that comes from training, practice, etc."[5] Most studies on skills intend the broadest interpretations of the term, including aptitude, behavior, ability, understanding, and flexibility. Skills usually encompass the abilities to think and innovate, to manage information, and to develop social and leadership connections. They involve both right- and left-brained thinking. In short, skill is the ability to do something well.

In the context of education, there are many different kinds of skills. Learning skills consist of knowing how to use knowledge and apply it to new situations; knowing how to analyze information and understand new ideas; knowing how to communicate and collaborate; and knowing how to solve problems, recognize patterns, and make decisions. Interpersonal skills involve the abilities to work on a team and be socially responsible, accountable, and self-starting; an aptitude for showing empathy and the ability to communicate are also vital interpersonal skills. Critical thinking skills are used for problem solving, making choices, appraising, and evaluating. Creativity, curiosity, predicting, and the ability to communicate new ideas are also extremely important critical thinking skills.

The Partnership for 21st Century Skills has compiled an outline of learning skills from studies done by a wide range of educational and research associations (page 9, Figure 1.1). The Partnership has broken the skills into categories and added brief explanations of how these skills play out in action. Their thinking—and ours—is that the important core subjects students learn must be accompanied by the teaching of these skills.

The belief that students must develop skills more relevant to the various changes occurring worldwide does not necessarily mean that what teachers have been teaching has been for naught—not at all. What it does suggest is that a new model of education is necessary, one that integrates the old skills with the new, including the higher-level thinking skills required to successfully negotiate contemporary life. In developing such an approach, educators may find themselves desirous of extending their own higher-level thinking skills as well. Questions for Life provides a model for teachers to use in enhancing these skills in themselves and developing them in their students.

Why do we need a new approach? Traditional curriculum teaches specific core subjects: math, science, history, English, reading or language arts, geography, economics, fine arts, foreign languages, etc.

INFORMATION AND COMMUNICATION SKILLS	**INFORMATION AND MEDIA LITERACY SKILLS** Analyzing, accessing, managing, integrating, evaluating, and creating information in a variety of forms and media; understanding the role of media in society.
	COMMUNICATION SKILLS Understanding, managing, and creating effective oral, written, and multimedia communication in a variety of forms and contexts.
THINKING AND PROBLEM-SOLVING SKILLS	**CRITICAL THINKING AND SYSTEMS THINKING** Exercising sound reasoning in understanding and making complex choices; understanding the interconnections between systems.
	PROBLEM IDENTIFICATION, FORMULATION, AND SOLUTION Framing, analyzing, and solving problems.
	CREATIVITY AND INTELLECTUAL CURIOSITY Developing, implementing, and communicating new ideas to others; staying open and responsive to new and diverse perspectives.
INTERPERSONAL AND SELF-DIRECTIONAL SKILLS	**INTERPERSONAL AND COLLABORATIVE SKILLS** Demonstrating teamwork and leadership; adapting to varied roles and responsibilities; working productively with others; exercising empathy; respecting diverse perspectives.
	SELF-DIRECTION Monitoring one's own understanding and learning needs; locating appropriate resources; transferring learning from one domain to another.
	ACCOUNTABILITY AND ADAPTABILITY Exercising personal responsibility and flexibility in personal, workplace, and community contexts; setting and meeting high standards and goals for oneself and others; tolerating ambiguity.
	SOCIAL RESPONSIBILITY Acting responsibly with the interests of the larger community in mind; demonstrating ethical behavior in personal, workplace, and community contexts.

Adapted from the work of the American Library Association, Association of College and Research Libraries, The Big6, Center for Media Literacy, Educational Testing Service, National Skill Standards Board, North Central Regional Education. Laboratory's enGauge, and the Secretary's Commission on Achieving Necessary Skills (SCANS). Partnership for 21st Century Skills (2006). *Learning for the 21st Century: A Report and MILE Guide for 21st Century Skills.*

Figure 1.1

These subjects are taught with the intention and assumption that their content will be applied in what we often call "real life": arenas, such as law, medicine, technology, business, sports, government, and family life, that lie beyond the classroom. However, do the critical thinking skills required to learn these subject matters ever become the focus of the lesson? In most cases, they are never mentioned.

Implicit in the teaching of Shakespeare, for example, is the assumption that students will gain an understanding of archetypes that they can apply to future life situations. *Implicit* and *assumption* are the operative words here because so often a discussion about archetypes per se never takes place.

Another example is math. Math skills are usually taught in the context of solving problems in a textbook. If these skills were applied instead to real-life situations, such as balancing a checkbook or estimating revenue from a paper route, they would generate more interest because students would realize that what they were learning had a direct impact on their daily lives.

When a skill central to the thinking process is not specifically taught, students may incidentally pick it up, but they will fail to develop an understanding of how it relates to the thinking process. Yet this relationship is an important link that teaches students how to apply the skill in other situations.

The same may be true for educators. For example, using prior experience and the power of observation to identify which students might pass a test involves thinking skills nearly identical to those used in selecting ingredients for a special meal. Understanding what skills are used not only allows us to apply them to other situations, it provides an opportunity to use them in purposeful ways, to form strategies that will help us solve problems, create lesson plans, or make decisions.

On page 12 Figure 1.2 shows the Questions for Life model. Using shapes and cue words explained later in this book, the Questions for Life model identifies 11 thinking processes we use continuously in our daily lives. The skills central to these processes can be applied to the compilation of twenty-first-century learning skills found in Figure 1.1 on page 9.

Change: An Opportunity

Given that world changes are very real and that they will keep on coming in ever-expanding ways, education has no choice but to evolve. Cultural changes alone will transform education. Students may be preparing for jobs that have not yet been invented, and they will certainly be involved with products and services that, if Daniel Pink is right, will far surpass past innovations. Students will be interacting globally on a daily basis with people from other cultures speaking differing languages, and they will be constantly improving ways to connect and share information.

It is difficult to know exactly which current core subjects will be most important in the future; nor can we predict to what ends they will be used. For these reasons we need to transform education by redirecting our emphasis to a focus on thinking itself—on thinking skills in the broadest sense and on how students can apply those skills in real-life contexts. Doing so will provide the basic tools both students and teachers need to do well in any subject or activity.

Rather than look at changes as a threat or an obstacle, we can see them as an opportunity to make schools the ideal laboratories for developing sound thinking patterns in people who can achieve great mental acuity and flexibility as they go forward to meet whatever lies ahead.

In Chapter 2 we will explore how an approach to schools that encompasses important life skills, critical thinking, and questioning strategies can prepare both students and educators for the fast-paced and exciting world in which we all now live.

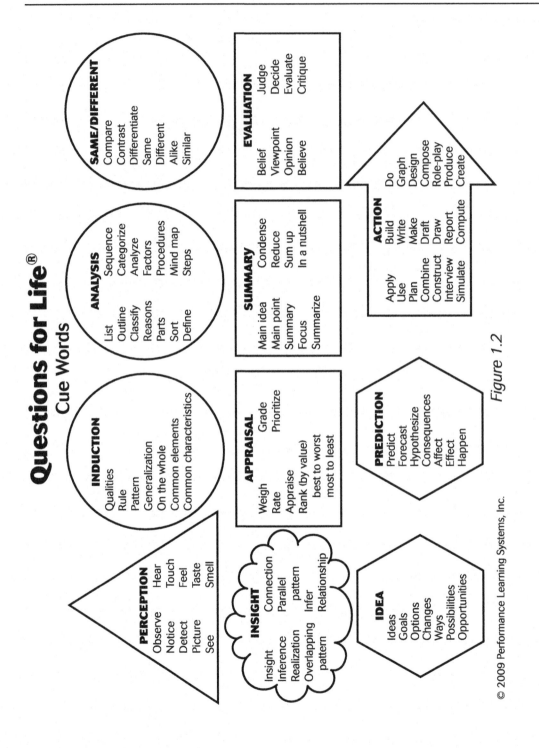

Questions for Life®
Cue Words

SAME/DIFFERENT
Compare
Contrast
Differentiate
Same
Different
Alike
Similar

EVALUATION
Belief   Judge
Viewpoint   Decide
Opinion   Evaluate
Believe   Critique

ANALYSIS
List   Sequence
Outline   Categorize
Classify   Analyze
Reasons   Factors
Parts   Procedures
Sort   Mind map
Define   Steps

SUMMARY
Main idea   Condense
Main point   Reduce
Summary   Sum up
Focus   In a nutshell
Summarize

ACTION
Apply   Build   Do
Use   Write   Graph
Plan   Make   Design
Combine   Draft   Compose
Construct Draw   Role-play
Interview Report   Produce
Simulate   Compute   Create

INDUCTION
Qualities
Rule
Pattern
Generalization
On the whole
Common elements
Common characteristics

APPRAISAL
Weigh   Grade
Rate   Prioritize
Appraise
Rank (by value)
    best to worst
    most to least

PREDICTION
Predict
Forecast
Hypothesize
Consequences
Affect
Effect
Happen

PERCEPTION
Observe   Hear
Notice   Touch
Detect   Feel
Picture   Taste
See   Smell

INSIGHT
Insight   Connection
Inference   Parallel
Realization   pattern
Overlapping   Infer
  pattern   Relationship

IDEA
Ideas
Goals
Options
Changes
Ways
Possibilities
Opportunities

Figure 1.2

Chapter 2
How Critical Is
Critical Thinking?

Bags of Bark

To illustrate how skills are used in real life in ways that are different from how they're covered in classrooms, let's peek in on a beginning teacher who recently rented a house in the community where she is teaching. We'll call her Sarah.

Sarah found a cute little house to rent and was delighted with its backyard garden. Alas, the garden was adjacent to an unplanted area overcome with weeds. Sarah used a weed eater and then laid down black plastic over the weedy section, counting on the sun's heat to dry out the roots. She then intended to cover the area with redwood bark to nicely frame the garden.

The time arrived to purchase the bark. Sarah measured the area and found it was 13" by 4.5". She took her measurements to the garden section of a hardware store, where she discovered that the bark she wanted to buy was sold in bags of two cubic feet each.

Multiplying the length by the width, she calculated that her area was 58.5 square feet. That raised a question: How many cubic feet would she need to complete the job?

Sarah found a sales clerk and asked how many cubic feet of bark she needed to cover an area that was 58.5 square feet. "Oh, check with the paint department," he told her. "They know about these things."

"I was told you might know something about converting square feet to cubic feet," Sarah said to the sales clerk in the paint department.

"I can try," the clerk smiled.

"I'm not buying paint," Sarah explained apologetically. "I want to put bark down in my garden. They sell it in two-cubic-foot bags. I don't know how many bags I need to cover the area. Do you know anything about calculating cubic feet?" she asked.

"Well, a cubic foot is measured by adding up all four sides," he said with confidence.

Something in Sarah clicked. She seemed to recall a formula from somewhere in her distant past. "Don't you measure it by three?" she asked. "Height, width, length?"

"Well, picture a cubic foot," he replied. "It has four sides. You measure that and then just flatten it."

"Something tells me I need to divide by three."

"Maybe 3.14?" offered the clerk.

Still unsure but anxious to complete her errand, Sarah decided she would just guess at three bags and see how it went.

At the checkout, however, Sarah continued her quest. As an educator, she wanted to know the correct answer. "Do *you* know how to convert square feet to cubic feet?" she asked. "I have 58.5 square feet and am just guessing that these three bags of two cubic feet each will be enough."

The young checkout clerk's eyes glazed over. He was thinking back to some formula he had learned in school. He picked up his calculator and punched in some numbers, frowned, cleared it, and started over. "I used to know," he said. "There's a formula." Then he shrugged, handed her a pickup slip, and told her to pick the bags up in the back of the store.

Sarah drove around to Will Call at the back of the hardware store. A clerk greeted her and she handed him her pickup slip. As he started to get the bags, Sarah once again posed her question: "How many square feet are covered by two cubic feet of bark?"

"One bag covers a four-by-four area."

"How do you know that?" Sarah cried, delighted that someone had the answer.

"Because I ask customers who buy these bags to come back and let me know how far they go. They come back for more or come back to return them if they guessed wrong, and they tell me one bag covers about 16 square feet, if you're putting on only about an inch."

Sarah added one more bag of bark to her stack, paid for it, and drove away, happy with her purchase and her new knowledge.

What happened here is common. In order to come up with the information they needed, Sarah and the clerks were using memory skills to recall math formulas learned years before. But Sarah also used other skills in her attempt at problem solving. One of them was *picturing* her garden area as she used her perception to envision two cubic feet of bark separated into four sections and spread out on the area she wanted to cover. Another skill she used was *comparing* cubic feet to square feet. She also *analyzed, appraised, predicted,* and *communicated* with others. In the end, her answer came not from those relying on memory, but from someone who used the very important skill of Induction (a Questions for Life thinking process) to make a *generalization* based on the experiences—incidents—of others. (In a classroom, asking this clerk for the answer would be called cheating; in real life it's called collaboration.)

Had Sarah sought her information in a more strategic way, she might have chosen her questions differently. Better questions yield better responses. For example, who might know the answer from having had a similar experience? What ideas had been tried before? How could she have summarized her needs so the clerks could better understand her situation? Such questions could have led Sarah and the clerks into the type of thinking that would have better assisted them in finding the answer they sought.

As simple as this example might be, it illustrates how we all seem to fumble through life with only part of our thinking engaged. Sarah's decision was not crucial; she could have returned a bag if she'd bought too many or bought another if she had too few. But what if an important life decision had been at stake?

Critical Thinking

There is no common agreement on the meaning of *critical thinking*. It is often associated with math and the scientific method, but it does not mean thinking about or remembering facts or formulas. A problem-solving skill that applies to all disciplines and all aspects of life, it is a creative way of thinking that, with practice, enables us to make choices and decisions, resolve issues, and become responsible. Most notably, critical thinking relies on the ability to think independently, to make decisions based on reliable information, and to carry out those decisions responsibly.

Thinking about how many bags of bark cover a garden area, while important to the gardener, might be considered at the lower level of critical thinking. Thinking that is reflective, responsible, skillful, and focused on making decisions about what to do with our lives or what to believe can be considered a higher form of critical thinking. The following are examples of important questions this kind of thinking should address:

> How do I *weigh* when it is the right time to purchase a home or a car?

How can I *predict* whether to take the new job or a promotion?

How do we accurately *judge* the positions of various political candidates?

How can we *sum up* the ideas that go into determining the impacts of global warming?

Should we as a nation *decide* to use nuclear power? Why?

What are the *consequences* of maintaining integrity and self-respect if doing so means losing support from others?

How can I *analyze* the value of investing in a college education?

What *analytical* choices concerning life and death do I have if I am a juror in a murder trial?

Students, too, must apply critical thinking skills to make good decisions as they go through life:

How can I *analyze* ways to improve my math skills?

What *options* do I have when someone offers me drugs?

How can I *prioritize* what classes to focus on in high school?

How can I *weigh* whether to go to college or vocational school?

What *possibilities* do I have when I arrive at a party and don't know anyone? What should I *do*?

What *decisions* should I make about having sex?

In a nutshell, how can I handle a situation in which someone is bullying me?

What *ways* can I create to get other kids to like me?

What *focus* should I choose to post on my social networking site? What will the *consequences* be?

Two Prongs of a Tuning Fork

Education consists of two important and related aspects that can be likened to the two prongs of a tuning fork. The first attunes students to the content of important core subjects, imparting knowledge of *what* to think about. The second attunes them to ways to interpret, understand, evaluate, and apply that content to their lives—in short, it teaches them *how* to think. (See Figure 2.1) When these two aspects of education work together in an appropriate harmonious balance, they produce students who know how to turn well-considered information into meaningful action.

Education:

1. **Provides students with the content of important core subjects.**

2. **Offers students opportunities to apply that content to their lives.**

Figure 2.1

Faced with the increasing growth of available knowledge and a constant flood of information, standards, and mandates, teachers are hard-pressed to accomplish even the first prong of education, much less the second. Teachers and students have their energies so focused on imparting and acquiring the fundamental content of core subjects that they seldom have time to share, debrief, or reflect together before they have to press on to the next thing.

Yet the second prong of education offers a hugely important part of the learning process: figuring out how to think about content. This is *metacognition*—thinking about one's thinking, a process that entails critical thinking. If we know that our thinking process served us well in one decision-making, problem-solving, or creative endeavor, wouldn't we want to understand how the process worked so we could use it again in another situation?

Unfortunately, we seldom review that process, and even more seldom do we point it out to others as they are learning. In fact, the critical thinking piece—the second prong of education—is so often ignored that students don't even realize it's missing. The same may often be said of educators. Who has time to discuss how they came to a solution or a lesson-plan strategy when they're so busy managing knowledge, activities, and curriculum? How often do teachers engage in critical thinking by reflecting on how they arrived at a decision or a solution? We're hoping Questions for Life will provide the tool to help teachers and students begin to engage in that important part of learning, teaching, and living.

Once students absorb the information delivered by a teacher through a project or assignment and apply it successfully in follow-up exercises, they believe (and their teachers believe) that they have truly learned. Whether they can now go out into the world and apply the same thinking processes they understood for one or two assignments is another story. Without focusing on *how* they came to conclusions, gathered information, analyzed it, worked with it, and applied it successfully, students find it difficult to connect the thinking patterns they used to other situations, including some of the important ones that life throws their way.

Part of the resistance to change in education stems from the value placed on scholarly pursuits undertaken by an elite culture of gentlemen of wealth and position in the eighteenth and nineteenth centuries. Life moved a lot more slowly then, and scholars had time to ponder the ramifications of the literature they absorbed or debate the philosophical trends of their times. Now, although education has been largely modernized to accommodate more contemporary topics of interest, there lingers an almost romantic nostalgia for the days when parsing Chaucer, reading volumes of civics history, or poring over complex mathematical equations for the sheer mental exercise of doing so made up the sinew of a good education.

This group of scholars, however, faced challenges that were neither as complex nor as urgent as those we face today. While our reality insists that students need to get their minds around math, science, technology, and other disciplines in order to compete economically, it insists even more emphatically that they be able to apply the process of critical thinking to the knowledge they acquire. So yes, mental exercises in traditional disciplines are essential, but their framework has changed: now it is crucial that the thinking behind exercises be analyzed, understood, and applied to real life.

To think critically, we must be able to raise vital questions or pose problems and then organize our thinking clearly and precisely, in a way that suggests solutions. Critical thinking requires gathering information and using abstract ideas to interpret it. We need to come to well-reasoned conclusions or solutions, testing them against criteria and standards gathered for the purpose of understanding.

Critical thinking requires remaining open-minded, using alternative systems of thought, and being able to distinguish facts from opinions. It means being creative and having the mental resources to be confident in taking risks. It requires the abilities to distinguish what is practical from what is merely desirable and to discern who might be implicated in the consequences of an action.

Perhaps most importantly, critical thinking requires effective communication to support us in finding solutions to complicated problems and sharing them with others. In a fast-paced and complex world, connecting with others to discuss issues of common interest not only solves problems and makes individual lives less isolated but also benefits everyone by paving the way to a more peaceful planet. As we have seen, gone are the days of silo thinking and isolation within communities, races, cultures, and countries. We live in an inclusive environment in which it is increasingly important to think globally, collaboratively, and creatively in order to address what lies ahead. To adapt to oncoming changes and meet the challenges we face, we must have knowledge and skills beyond those that have traditionally served us.

From a fourth grader's point of view or from a middle school teacher's busy perspective, this talk of change and urgently needed new skills may seem daunting, to say the least. For educators grappling with mandated curriculum, nutrition, safety, discipline, counseling, social interactions, politics, and all the rest of what it means to be a teacher today, adaptation to a changing world may just seem to add another layer of obligation.

Shifting Perspective

Yet weary educators may take heart. There's a bright side to shifting the perspective of teaching from delivering knowledge to facilitating the recognition of one's own thinking processes. As students internalize the Questions for Life model, they acquire awareness of questions they can ask to develop their own critical thinking. Once they learn how to ask discerning questions, they are equipped to dive into problem solving on their own and to create solutions or arrive at answers that, yes, the teacher may not have exactly intended, but that are nevertheless the legitimate result of their own thought processes.

This thinking ability takes students out of the classroom and into the realm of real-life problems and concerns that sincerely engage them. In that environment the job of teaching becomes easier because students are learning and thinking on their own. And if students come up with an answer that is not the "right" one—not the intended one—the teacher has the tools to uncover their thinking process by using the Questions for Life model to debrief and perhaps guide them to a different answer.

Questions for Life was originally developed for educators when it was found that they were not making the connection between the type of thinking they understood in one staff development program and the similar type of thinking that was needed in another. They were not seeing, for example, that analysis they applied to a reading class was also applicable to a classroom management class. They had no common language for both of these applications. In the development of Questions for Life it was an easy move to take the model for teachers and apply it to students. Both benefit from investigating and understanding the thinking processes they use.

Teachers who readily employ Questions for Life in lesson planning have found that the critical thinking questions they design elicit answers that are more in-depth and reflective than ones they used to get before they understood and used the Questions for Life model. Rather than drawing blank stares in group discussions, teachers who ask questions from the model create a structure to elicit purposeful, meaningful communication based on inquiry that naturally causes students to think along certain pathways.

For instance, when each student in a cooperative learning group is given focused questions, group communication proceeds readily and enthusiastically, bypassing the usual problem of a few students dominating others who are hitchhiking onto the discussion. As students embrace the process, they know what to do to arrive at a summary, for example, or how to articulate why they arrived at a particular conclusion.

Likewise, students are able to respond to essay questions in ways that reflect thinking patterns inspired by familiarity with the cue words taken from the Questions for Life model. This process can be tailored to prepare students for college entrance exams. Additionally, student work in lab experiments and math assignments guided by questions using Questions for Life cue words shows the teacher what critical thinking processes students followed to arrive at their answers.

Teaching students how to think critically is like teaching them how to fish instead of merely giving them a fish. Empowering them to work with the Questions for Life model will transform them into people who can learn and work skillfully with others, collaborating on how the content of their learning plays out academically, socially, globally, and in every other aspect of their lives.

The model will also aid students in learning how to make sound decisions. Those who are incapable of making a decision or who make decisions using little forethought, unable to ask the kinds of questions that point to effective solutions, will be left behind to deal with the consequences. Questions for Life is a tool for decision making.

Providing students with the benefits of critical thinking requires teaching that will shift their perspective, but that is not as difficult as it may sound. There exist many schools, programs, and methods that reframe teaching to enable educators to help students internalize real-life skills as they acquire content and knowledge—with the major focus on skills, as content changes while skills essentially do not.

For example, here's how a third-grade teacher can work on reading by teaching her students what it means to summarize a story. *In a nutshell* is a cue word (or phrase) within the Questions for Life thinking strategy Summary. The teacher brings in a story on a sheet of paper and reads it with her students. She then asks, "*In a nutshell, what was the story about?*" She holds up an actual nutshell she has brought to class and proceeds to teach Summary by showing that the whole story will not go into the nutshell—attempts to fold the paper and cram it into the nutshell fail. But by identifying and literally cutting out and rolling up one or two main sentences or paragraphs—by condensing them, or summarizing the main points—they will fit nicely into the nutshell.

In Chapter 3 we'll visit teaching methods that develop critical thinking and look at how critical thinking skills benefit from questions designed to bring out learning in relevant, real-life situations. We'll see how debriefing what is learned can occur in all learning and in all situations that replicate life, even within the confines of a traditional classroom.

Chapter 3
How Tomorrow Learns

A New Focus

Charter and private schools with an approach to learning that encompasses real-life situations, critical thinking, and community involvement have popped up all across the country. Where resources and leadership allow, public schools are also opening to new curriculum or advances in technology that allow students to emerge from the confines of the lecture-based classroom into an arena where the stuff of schools begins to resemble the stuff of life.

The Bill and Melinda Gates Foundation[1] invests millions in preparing students for college, careers, and life itself. By encouraging schools across the country to focus on learning by doing and on applying knowledge to everyday life, the Foundation is helping to rethink schools. Its "3R's Solution" transforms the old "reading, writing, and 'rithmetic" to "rigor, relevance, and relationships."

Innovative high schools, in particular, are characterized by academically rigorous curriculums that offer project-based teaching and adapt course work to make it relevant to the real world. These schools offer a program-based, problem-based, or performance-based curriculum that uses classroom projects to address questions, issues, and technological concerns meaningful to students' everyday lives. The intent is to involve students in inquiry and deep learning that require critical thinking, self-direction, and communication with people in the larger community.

A couple of examples of such high schools within the United States are Metro High School[2] in Columbus, Ohio, and Chicago Public Schools Student Zone. Metro High was created in 2006 through a partnership between The Ohio State University and the Educational Council of Columbus, Ohio, and Battelle,[3] a scientific research think tank whose mission is to "translate scientific discovery into innovative solutions for the benefit of our fellow citizens, and to be a benefactor for charitable activities—especially education." The school is small and its curriculum emphasizes four subjects: science, technology, engineering, and math, to which they have applied the acronym STEM.

Students are chosen to attend Metro by lottery, which creates a diverse population with a cross section of cultures. There is no tuition. Freedom and flexibility reign, and the school has no bells, lockers, or schedules. The catch is that students need to meet 90 percent of the requirements developed—they have to get A's to receive credit.

While the purpose of Metro High is to prepare students for success in college, it focuses on giving eleventh and twelfth graders opportunities to practice hands-on, self-directed learning outside the classroom with teachers and mentors from the community. Students learn by doing. "Lectures are an extremely inefficient way to teach students," states Robert Perry, a professor at the school and a parent of one of the students. Specifically, students learn through:

- Independent research projects.
- Group projects with other students.
- Community internships at "learning centers" in the community.

At Chicago's Student Zone,[4] a prime example of project-based learning, students are initially asked, "What do *you* want to learn?" Their projects are live, real, and out in the world. Collaboration, teachable moments, and interaction with the community provide the cornerstone of the school's educational focus.

K–12 students are not the only ones who are meeting reality head-on and learning how to change their approach to learning. Daniel Pink, writing about the need to be more collaborative and right-brain-directed, notes enthusiastically that the "curriculum at American medical schools is undergoing its greatest change in a generation." He cites as an example students at Columbia University Medical School who are undertaking "narrative medicine," a practice that helps them to communicate better with patients by listening to their stories. Students at Yale School of Medicine are studying painting to hone their perception skills and thus their ability to notice subtle details in their patients. These skills go beyond clinical, diagnostic thinking to a kind of thinking that involves perception, comparison, and induction (similar to the thinking processes in Questions for Life).

Beyond our borders a focus on thinking takes top priority. At Olentangy High School in Finland, where all teachers are required to have master's degrees, educators enjoy complete freedom with school curriculum. The goal is to encourage students to think for themselves, a reflection of the Finns' conviction that today's students represent their country's future. At the same time, university entrance exams are very rigorous. Students who qualify can attend college tuition-free. The dropout rate at Olentangy High School is less than one percent.

In Aruba, a small Dutch island in the Caribbean, a ten-year vision for educating students focuses as much on good citizenship as on scholarly pursuits. Education is intended to create students who are global thinkers, who can communicate well in four languages, and who display proficiency in technical, communication, and social skills.

Developed by focus groups made up of students, parents, educators, and other community members, the Strategic National Education Plan from the Ministry of Education in Aruba[5] lists desired student achievement under categories that include:

Thinking and Learning Skills:
Demonstrating effective communication
Working on a team
Using initiative
Thinking creatively

Life Skills:
Demonstrating leadership by mobilizing others, using
   interpersonal and problem-solving skills
Applying knowledge to practical endeavors
Showing effective, efficient work habits
Demonstrating ambition, a positive mental attitude,
   self-confidence, adaptability, accountability, integrity, and
   social responsibility

ICT Literacy:
Information and communications technology

Knowledge:
Demonstrating awareness of global issues
Participating in practices that promote health, fitness,
   and well-being

These skills, behaviors, qualities, and attitudes reflect parallel skills developed independently in the United States by Partnership for 21st Century Skills,[6] listed in Figure 1.1 on page 9 in Chapter 1.

Other project-based or problem-based schools work toward the same end—offering opportunities for students to engage in live or at least simulated projects that will help them make connections between what they learn in school and what is happening in the outside world.

The Future of Work

James P. Ware and Charles Grantham cofounded a research and advisory firm called Work Design Collaborative that manages The Future of Work, a collaborative organization dedicated to creating and implementing new ways to work effectively in the modern world. The Future of Work assists global organizations in accommodating many current changes, including, for example, changes due to technology and the need for more green businesses, traffic mitigation, and holding global meetings. Ware and Grantham also authored *Corporate Agility,*[7] a book that encourages corporations to allow employees more freedom to choose where they will work, whether in the office, from home, or in a "third place" (i.e., a place other than the home or office), which stimulates creativity and innovation.

When asked what critical thinking skills future students should know for tomorrow's workplace, Ware referred to the types of skills learned in math and science: evidence-based thinking, logic, the scientific method, and hypothesis formation.[8] All of these skills are built on abilities that include prediction, data comprehension, analysis, distinguishing fact from opinion, and formulating good questions. Critical thinking is highly systematic, and like any system, it follows a flow, or a path, as it moves along in a series of interconnected questions and answers that eventually develop into a decision or a plan.

In the real world most questions deserve more than pat answers—one must use a process of skilled critical thinking to come up with appropriately useful, thoughtful, and responsive answers. To survive, according to Jim Ware, students must be "architects" of thinking, able to build their own conclusions based on their own thought processes.

How can educators reframe their teaching techniques to help students acquire the skilled thinking processes they will need to perform the work of the future? "Begin immediately with performance-based learning," Ware suggests. "Give students responsibility for literally cleaning up the classroom at the elementary level, and move to collaborating with the teacher on how or what to learn in later grades. Debrief everything you do and connect the learning with real life."

He continues: "Teachers need to create real-life lessons, and students need to be involved with real tasks for real people. They need to see that what they do makes a difference and has a consequence, that it counts, and that it deals with reality."

Live Events

Real-life lessons—or live events, as we prefer to call them—are learning activities or actions that have some consequence in reality. They count. They typically involve the emotions and the senses, and they always hold relevance or meaning for students. Often teams are created, collaboration takes place, relationships are formed, and presentations are made to the public.

Some live events are more complex and have more meaning or relevance than others. Some are quiet, simple events. Some are exciting, busy, noisy, and fun. In the best of all possible worlds, we would be living each moment with aliveness, finding rich meaning, emotional satisfaction, and profound learning in everything we do. That is how we live when we are having a wonderful day, when the world is at our feet. That is what is always available to us—and to our students—when we make the time and create the environment to notice.

Some live events take on an existence of their own. A live event, for example, might center on the plight of the homeless as students visit a homeless shelter. Their experience might inspire them to initiate and manage a coat drive. Within that activity (as within every student plan, observation, or sentiment) lie opportunities to implant learning, from studying economics and social behaviors to writing publicity and doing the simple math involved in counting and distributing coats. Through questioning and debriefing as the event unfolds, teachers and students have opportunities to make real-life connections. The live event may have started simply as one lesson plan, one unit of study on the homeless, but fueled by real student interest, the coat drive might continue every year, long after the first students have completed their lesson.

The role of educators when teaching live events is to make students aware of the learning as it unfolds by helping them identify exactly what goes on in their thinking process, and why.

Briefing and Debriefing Live Events

Live events need to be briefed and debriefed. During the briefing process, which occurs before and during the activity, the teacher lets students know what to look for, giving them a summary and pertinent instructions or information about what might occur in the live event. Using Questions for Life, the educator can prompt or guide students' thinking so they will observe, generate ideas, or use other desired thinking processes as they work. For example, the teacher may set up the live event by asking, "What are you going to look for?" and "What steps will you be taking?" Using the questioning strategies for planning helps a teacher focus and keep the lesson on track. And it allows a teacher to address learning styles: global and sequential, analytical and creative.

By sharing with students the process used to prepare for a live event, including how and why particular questioning strategies were developed, the teacher can model how to plan and develop strategic thinking. This kind of transparency allows students to learn how to become aware of and develop their own thinking processes—and this, in a nutshell, provides students with the skills and knowledge they need in order to become lifelong learners. (Teachers would do well to point this out to their students, since lifelong learning, while often touted as something we should all strive for, seldom gets explained.) Opening up the thinking process empowers both teacher and student, and allows the juices to flow. In that open environment far more real learning occurs than in a closed, rigid situation in which students are struggling to get one "right" answer or find one "right" solution.

A good example of this transparency occurs in science experiments set up by teachers who explain the teaching process and then let the experiments further the learning on their own. Teachers, of course, know and understand the ideas behind what they want their students to learn—slicing these larger ideas into smaller pieces of learning constitutes the backbone of good teaching. But sharing the big picture of what the teacher wants students to pick up in their slice of learning also augments the learning and encourages student buy-in.

An example of briefing a live event might occur when a group of middle school students who have been studying their district's court system actually sit in on a courtroom hearing for someone who was arrested for driving under the influence. Students have been briefed on the DUI law and its consequences and have had a look at the roles various people play in a court hearing: bailiff, judge, attorney, defendant, and witnesses.

In explaining the court process, the teacher suggests that students pay attention to what they observe and perceive. The teacher encourages them to take notes on what they are thinking about the case and to formulate questions in their minds as the event unfolds: What do I see? How do I feel about the courtroom environment? How do I think the hearing might end?

At the conclusion of the live event, the students connect what they learned about the situation as it was set up for them and what actually happened as the situation unfolded. The teacher had briefed students on what *might* occur in the courtroom, but the nature of live events is that they unfold in a variety of unpredictable ways. This lived experience provides a powerful teaching moment: solid critical thinking takes place as students compare and contrast what they anticipated from criteria established ahead of the event (the briefing) with what actually occurred (the debriefing).

The debriefing process often elicits learning that may not have been obvious, and this is why questioning strategies are crucial. For example, the following questions and ones like them can lead students to reflect upon, summarize, and come to conclusions about what they experienced: "What decisions did you make? How would you evaluate this situation? What action should we take?" And not only do students learn the content in question, they also learn about learning as they consciously consider what thinking processes led them to their conclusions.

While debriefing the teachable moment has traditionally been the role of teachers, facilitators, or coaches, it can also be the role of students themselves when they learn the structure of the Questions for Life questioning strategies and cue words. Once students learn how to look for learning in life—how to ask questions and go through the thinking process that leads to learning—they can debrief learning in everything.

Another way to debrief a live event occurs when the event unfolds in the process of life itself: a community meeting takes place, a call is placed to another country, a chemical reaction explodes, a wounded bird flies into the classroom, a student develops and delivers a PowerPoint presentation. There are endless learning opportunities in life! During or after the event, the teacher can pose questions and elicit thought processes using the Questions for Life cue words, which solidify the learning, whether in content or process skills. After the community meeting, for example, the teacher might debrief using Questions for Life cue words (shown in italics) in the following ways: "*List* the three points the presenter made about the political issues surrounding the school's expansion" (Analysis), "*Summarize* the main points made by the person objecting to the project" (Summary), "*Contrast* this political system to the one that exists in Germany" (Same/Different), "*Evaluate* how well you think the presenter made her case" (Evaluation).

Teachers can help students doing presentations to debrief themselves as presenters: "What did you *notice* in the audience as you presented?" (Perception), "How would you *rate* your performance on a scale of 1 to 10?" (Appraisal). And the teacher can also debrief the audience: "What did you *notice* about the presenter's body language?" (Perception), "How was this presenter's message the *same* and how was it *different* from the one we had last week?" (Same/Different).

As described above, the teacher elicits the learning before, during, and after the event by posing questions and guiding students to observe or appraise, evaluate, or gain insight. Had students previously learned about Questions for Life, the ensuing discussion would have been that much more enriched.

Using the Questions for Life Model

The Questions for Life model helps teachers to formulate the right questions to ask—the stimulating questions that generate real thinking and uncover the learning that occurred. Developing questions from the model also assists in an intervention situation, as teachers can hone in on what they really want to learn about their students and identify what steps to take to assist in their learning.

Asking questions with embedded Questions for Life cue words is the process for using the Questions for Life model. Each cue word stimulates a different thinking process in the brain; *comparing* (Same/Different), for example, calls for a thinking process that is different from *rating* (Appraisal).

Teachers who use the Questions for Life model often place the cue words in posters around the classroom for easy reference. They can point to the thinking processes relevant to whatever content they happen to be addressing during the day, showing their students the flow of systematic critical thinking.

Teachers can also use Questions for Life to develop lesson plans whose efficacy is improved by the model's ability to enhance differentiated instruction. As teachers gather information for developing a lesson plan, they look at the data and identify how they will solicit the learning they are seeking. They map out the questions they want to pose to the different levels of students in their class. Those who are hesitant to participate in analyzing a subject, for example, can be asked questions that go back to their perceptions—"What do you see? What do you feel?"—and be emboldened to move out from there. Each student may arrive at an answer or a solution by a different path, but each answer will be valid if guided by questions that support the student's individual thinking.

Critical Thinking for Students and Educators

But wait. It's asking a lot of an educator to teach curriculum, focus on learning standards, plan live-event lessons, and elicit critical thinking. Furthermore, it's highly possible that teachers themselves may not recognize what learning or critical thinking occurs during a live event. They may be unconvinced that a student's thinking process really *was* critical or that such thinking alone signified that any learning took place. This may all seem too fuzzy: thinking is one thing—acing the test and meeting the standard is another. And it is this "other," giving tests and meeting standards, that educators are accustomed to providing.

Another challenge in this mix is the fact that some teachers may also be unaware of their own thinking and may now be questioning whether they are, in fact, critical thinkers. Being an adult does not automatically provide us with that skill. Fortunately, however, it is one that can be learned and taught. The cue words used in Questions for Life trigger awareness of thought processes (metacognition) in *everyone,* whether they are students, teachers, or people in other walks of life. This awareness empowers them to practice the thinking skills they already use, but which they may not have identified or articulated as thinking processes. Because Questions for Life is brain-compatible (i.e., it both follows and elicits our natural thinking patterns), practicing and internalizing its use need not be a grueling task. It really boils down to awareness followed by practice, just as any learning does.

As teachers endeavor to reframe teaching to focus on real-life situations and tasks, they can rely on the Questions for Life process of briefing and debriefing to let them know that students are thinking in real time about real things. Likewise, teachers can rely on the process when they themselves need to make decisions, create strategies, and find solutions to real-life problems. Once teachers become accustomed to using the process, they turn to it naturally as they teach, interact with others, promote ideas, write grants, develop relationships—in short, participate in all the different aspects of an educator's life. Teachers, too, live in the real world and need real-life skills.

Chapter 4
How Do We Get
There From Here?

Questioning Strategies

The role of the educator seems to grow exponentially: teacher leads to disciplinarian leads to counselor leads to nutritionist! The list goes on—administrative duties, working with personal coaches, community involvement, mentoring new teachers, managing IT, or becoming the default director of the upcoming play.

But above all, educators are strategists. Consciously or unconsciously, teachers strategize when they develop lesson plans, seek peer coaching, or take part in team teaching. Strategies come constantly into play as teachers manage the school day, head off bullying behavior, or lead multicultural and multilingual classrooms. In fact, most of what teachers do in every aspect of their lives involves strategies—navigating all kinds of situations and decisions, choosing a path to get to where they want to go, and deciding on options to solve problems.

Questioning strategies are the educator's mainstay. Whether to influence student behavior; assess student understanding; determine the needs of parents, students, or administrators; or pose reflective inquiries of themselves, teachers use questioning as a life raft for getting through the complexities of any given day. Questions are designed to probe for further information, enhance understanding, and generate student thinking. As a strategy, questioning is as old as Socrates, who initiated its systematic use to stimulate critical thinking.

To successfully integrate the requirements of twenty-first-century learning with the skills taught in schools, questioning strategies must clearly focus more on the thinking process itself than on ascertaining whether or not students "got" information. A shift in how questions are designed and posed is in order, one that calls for students to analyze their thinking, gain insight from it, and apply it to their lives.

A Revised Taxonomy

When Benjamin Bloom's Taxonomy of Educational Objectives was developed in the early 1950s, it became the mainstay of sequenced instruction for teachers. In 2001 several of Bloom's former students revised and updated the taxonomy, having shown that teaching skills sequentially, building one upon another, is an ineffective way to create understanding.[1] In fact, as they discovered, students learn skills simultaneously in a random order.

Bloom focused on various types of questions used in teaching, whereas Questions for Life focuses on the thinking processes embedded in the questions. The old taxonomy claimed students needed to comprehend information before applying it; the new taxonomy suggests that they can be applying, analyzing, or working with information before fully understanding its content. In other words, they can begin working on processes and move backward to comprehension. For example, they can observe and synthesize a project before analyzing what needs to be done, or they can evaluate a Web site before they have any knowledge about what it represents. Science education best reflects this way of working with information: students experience the process and then go back to make connections to knowledge.

How does a teacher question to determine understanding in this situation? How can a student's knowledge be successfully assessed? Clearly, such an assessment requires a new approach. It calls for new questioning strategies and a reframing of how educators use their own critical thinking and facilitation skills to step away from the teacher-student hierarchy and work more collaboratively with students to guide them in developing their own thinking skills, regardless of content.

Even the language of teaching could stand to change direction. In referring to a planned lesson, project, or activity for students, teachers often use terminology such as "I will have them," "make them," "tell them," or "get them" to learn or work in certain ways. Just as managers in business and other organizations today can no longer manipulate employees in these ways, teachers can no longer assume that students will willingly follow along or participate in their plans. In both cases, technology and access to information that is transparent and ubiquitous has caused a flattening of the old manipulative top-down style.

In short, to "get" students to think, educators must alter their strategy. And strategy, of course, cannot be undertaken without a goal—a desired outcome or result. Believing that the goal is achievable puts real power behind the strategy.

Goals

So often we set goals for students that we secretly believe many of them will not achieve. Without believing in the possible achievement of our articulated goals (even if they differ for each student), the outcome falls apart—for everyone. This is true because moving toward a goal we consider unachievable causes tension and dissatisfaction. If we move toward the goal anyway, hoping for the best, our self-limiting belief about its achievement holds us back; at the same time, we can't help but be pulled the other way by our natural desire to fulfill the goal. Meaningful goals and beliefs are aligned and congruent, offering unambivalent support to outcomes that may then develop freely.

Card Game Strategies

Imagine playing a game of cards. You have a deck with four suits: spades, hearts, diamonds, and clubs. You have cards numbered from 1 (ace) to 10. All cards are either black or red, and some are face cards showing pictures representing jacks, queens, and kings.

Let's say you are dealt a hand of ten cards in a game of gin rummy.[2] The strategy is to combine most of your cards into sets and runs and keep the point value of your remaining unmatched cards low so you can achieve the goal, which is to win the game.

There are two piles of cards placed side by side on the table between you and your partner—a stockpile and a discard pile. The discard pile shows cards faceup so you can see them; the stockpile is facedown. You take a card from either pile and decide to keep it to make your sets and runs or to discard it to the faceup pile; your partner may then choose to pick it up or take one from the facedown stockpile.

Your decisions about whether to use a card or not, how to arrange it in your hand, whether to pull from the discard pile or the stockpile, and how to play your hand to lower leftover points constitute your strategies. You are thinking constantly about the value of the cards, what values or suits your partner has picked up, how much time has passed, whether to break up a set to try for a run, and what risks to take to try to win the game.

Let's say that you did win the game and are now going to play a hand of five-card-draw poker. Your goal here is to win money! And you win money by betting that you have a better hand than any of your opponents have (sometimes players choose to bluff, pretending their hands are better than they really are, but that's another topic . . .). You are dealt five cards; you observe them and predict whether or not you can discard some in order to make a better hand. You are allowed to discard up to four cards, receiving four new ones from the dealer. You analyze your hand and arrange it in a way to achieve the highest rank.

Got that?

What was the same and what was different about those two games? You used the same materials, but each game called for different strategies, depending on the goal. Obviously, educational and life goals entail strategies of greater consequence than those used in card games (unless you're a professional poker player, in which case the strategies may be of very significant consequence!).

Strategizing to Reach a Goal

Really, a strategy is nothing more than a plan to achieve a goal. A strategy constitutes a hypothesis showing cause and effect: if we do this, then that might happen. It takes us from a present position to a desirable but uncertain future position. Strategies often require trade-offs—choices about what *not* to do are as important as choices about what *to* do—and they involve various thought processes, both conceptual and analytical.

Strategies promote action by improving our decision-making focus: decisions that are inconsistent with furthering a proposed strategy can be rejected. Sometimes we can change a strategy to make it consonant with a decision, which is fine as long as both are consistent with the goal. The goal, too, may be changed, though typically, changing strategies is more achievable.

Strategies can enhance performance for the same reason. We can ask: "Is what we are doing in keeping with our strategy? If not, let's not do it." This fine-tunes performance, keeping it on track.

Teaching Strategies

Strategizing can be simple or it can involve sophisticated, subtle, and sometimes unconscious elements of thinking. But it does involve thinking. In education, it involves thinking critically about a way to frame teaching so that educator and student alike can participate in an agreed-upon strategy and learn how to apply the learning, both immediately and in the long term. If a student comes up with an idea, for example, the teacher can help the student look at all the aspects of that idea by doing an analysis and perhaps by making a prediction.

As another example, a teacher may fully intend to employ a teaching strategy using technology familiar to students in order to support the research on a given topic. The teacher thinks through the process of thinking that would be involved in this endeavor and then bravely shares it with a first-year high school student. If they have experienced earlier collaboration and developed a trusting relationship, the student may hear out the teacher's approach and then gently suggest a shortcut, a different avenue, or a new technology that would do the job better. Together they can argue about or agree upon the thinking processes that lead to the learning and in the process develop a closer relationship and enjoy an experience of lifelong learning (which is talked about at length in education but never really incorporated in traditional top-down teaching).

Similarly, the Questions for Life model offers a tool to strategize questioning in a way that generates student thinking. When it is used transparently, both student and teacher look at the various questioning strategies and collaborate on how best to arrive at a conclusion or a solution. This can be done individually or together—or both. Reframing education from a knowledge-transmitting model to one that elicits thinking and curiosity can engage students in deciding for themselves how they want to map a path to the learning that they themselves decide they want to acquire. But what comes first is the shift in how a teacher thinks about thinking.

Questions for Life provides an opportunity for educators to use inquiry to determine their own thinking processes in both their personal and professional lives. And as teachers tend to do, they can transfer their experience and understanding of questioning strategies and thinking to their students.

Questions for Life assists not only teachers but anyone who wishes to focus on how best to arrive at sound decisions, come to accurate conclusions, and create strategies that meet goals. These abilities become hugely important when applied to life's big decisions. Questions for Life really means what it says—asking the right questions can develop astute critical thinking about life in general and one's own life in particular. Educators who have that inner passion for life, who seek learning not only for their students but for themselves, are at the core of sound teaching: they learn for themselves and impart learning to others, solidifying their own learning in the process.

Steven Wolk, associate professor in the Teacher Education Department at Northeastern Illinois University in Chicago and a regular contributor to *Phi Delta Kappan* magazine, states in his article "School as Inquiry":

> The best teachers I know aren't good just because of what they do in their classrooms for six hours a day; they're good teachers because of how they live their lives 24 hours a day. These teachers live a life filled with learning, thinking, reading,

and debating. Because inquiry is an important part of their lives, inquiry becomes an essential part of their classroom.[3]

In the chapters that follow we will look at the practical application of the Questions for Life model. We'll see how its various shapes, cue words, and questioning strategies work to elicit thinking that leads to solutions, decisions, creative endeavors, and reflection.

In short, we'll deal the cards!

Chapter 5
The Questions for Life Model

Looking Back: A Brief Summary

In this book we have looked at how the wave of changes coming to education from global transformation creates strongly compelling reasons to improve learning and critical thinking skills in our schools. We have also looked at what critical thinking represents, how it plays out in our lives in terms of economic and professional advancement, and how it contributes to fulfillment in our personal lives, whether we are educators or students. We noted some places around the country and the world that are implementing techniques to develop higher-level thinking and real-life learning. We took a look at how strategy plays an important role in teaching and how reframing strategies to encompass questioning and real-life learning can enhance students' and teachers' abilities to think critically and well.

In summary, we've presented the value of the Questions for Life model to interest you in learning how to use this and other models to meet challenges and improve strategies that will advance education.

Rather than simply providing the Questions for Life model as yet another technique to try out in the classroom for a period or two, we have endeavored to instill a value for developing questioning and critical thinking skills in everyday life in order to improve decision-making and problem-solving abilities. As you internalize your own critical thinking skills, you can naturally model and transmit them to your students.

Gone are the days when the all-knowing teacher planned lessons in private, delivered them from a podium, and hoped the struggling student would grasp the point and cross the threshold of under-standing. To be effective and aligned with advances in technology and global diversity, today's teaching must be transparent. Neither teacher nor parent can toss around the old adage, "Do as I say, not as I do"—students are too savvy for that. A better approach now is for teachers to model the model: to use questioning and critical thinking strategies in their own lives and in their teaching so students can see the value and follow their lead.

Questions and Statements

Research continues to show that most of the questions teachers pose each day are memory questions. Thus, most classroom think-ing takes place at the recall or recognition level instead of at the level of critical thinking. Educators who have received training in asking higher-level questions and who employ that level of thinking in their everyday lives ask fewer recall questions and more critical thinking questions. In doing so, they create a significant increase in student achievement.

The Questions for Life model asks questions that all of us raise in real-life situations involving both our professional and private lives. It takes some practice to master using these questions, particularly if one is accustomed to posing mostly memory-level questions, but the task is made easier by the fact that critical thinking questions—Questions for Life—are brain-compatible, flowing along the lines that the brain naturally follows. Being aware of the type of questions or thinking we are engaged in helps to clarify and crystallize our thinking. In fact, Questions for Life provides an opportunity to expand thinking and questioning strategies to include higher-level questions.

Questions for Life can be asked as questions or given as directives or statements. We prefer the term *statement* to indicate a move away from the traditional top-down, teacher-student hierarchy implied by a "directive." So a statement requesting Analysis thinking might be, "*List* the two types of city government." An Analysis statement for younger students might be, "Give the *steps* for cleaning the hamster cage and the *reasons* for doing each step."

Because Questions for Life elicits deeper thinking, questioning strategies often do not require one exact right answer; Evaluation, Induction, Insight, and other thought processes vary with the individual, depending on how he or she perceives or processes the question or statement. Of course, there are also many times when there *is* a right answer, as in the case of a response to a request for a specific physical property in a Perception question: "*Observe* this pencil. What color is the shaft? What is its texture?"

It's also true that whenever someone spends time perceiving data, analyzing it, arriving at inductions, and then moving back again to perception, he or she is better equipped to make sound evaluations, summaries, and predictions. The first row of the Questions for Life model sets the stage for moving to the second and third rows.

Questions for Life Shapes and Cue Words

Refer again to Figure 1.2, on page 12 in Chapter 1, the Questions for Life Cue Words chart (you can also tear out or look at the perforated card with the same information at the back of this book). The chart shows thinking processes and terms to use when selecting questions or statements intended to elicit certain types of thinking in ourselves or others.

Notice there are three rows of *thinking processes* and their associated critical thinking skills and questioning strategies. The first row consists of four basic kinds of thinking processes: Perception, Induction, Analysis, and Same/Different. The next two rows cover more complex thinking processes: Insight, Appraisal, Summary, and Evaluation in the second row and Idea, Prediction, and Action in the third row. In all, there are 11 different processes, each enclosed in a particular shape. Each one is elicited in our thinking by the cue words associated with it. The cue word lists are not exhaustive—other words can be thought of that also invoke the various processes. But the Questions for Life cue words represent an ample number of ways teachers can trigger the thinking processes they want their students to use.

Geometric Shapes

Notice on the Questions for Life Cue Words card (or in Figure 1.2) that the thinking processes (or questioning strategies) are represented by various geometric shapes. Perception, for example, is represented as a triangle in the first row of the chart. Within each shape, a thinking process name tops a list of other words or phrases. The shapes that surround each thinking process depict each one; some are similar in nature, others quite different. You will see these shapes used in various graphics throughout the book, and we will focus on a more in-depth description of what they represent in Chapter 8 when we see how the various thinking processes move and flow.

You might think of these shapes as similar to the cards in our card game example, where we had hearts, diamonds, clubs, spades, and face cards, each with its own meaning or value.

Cue Words

Below each questioning strategy or process name and within each shape are the *cue words* we referred to earlier. These words signal to the person being questioned what type of thinking he or she should use to formulate a response. For example, if you ask students about the *qualities* of something, you will see on the chart that you are asking them to respond using the thinking process Induction; hence you are asking an Induction question.

The key to using the Questions for Life model is to incorporate the cue words as often as possible in order to trigger the brain processes you are seeking. This may seem awkward at first, but continued practice with the cue words soon allows you and your students to associate each cue word with its corresponding thinking process, enabling everyone to move more naturally from one thought process to another. Allowing a pause before students are required to give an answer gives them time to make the mental transition to the thinking process embedded in or indicated by the question. Thinking aloud is a way teachers can model using cue words to indicate what thinking process they used to arrive at an answer. Very often it is helpful for students to "hear" the process of thinking.

Open-Ended Questions

Whereas closed-ended questions elicit short, yes-or-no responses that serve to answer recall questions, open-ended questions tend to broaden information-gathering opportunities and generate more thinking. It is important that higher-level questions, at least, be asked as open-ended questions to bring forth deeper, more complex thoughts and feelings. For example, the question "When did the United States drop atomic bombs over Hiroshima and Nagasaki?" is a closed-ended recall question. To elicit students' knowledge, understanding, and thoughts about that event, the teacher should use such open-ended questions as (cue words are shown in italics): "What *beliefs* do you have about that event?" (Evaluation), "What *options* besides dropping the atomic bombs might the United States have had?" (Idea).

Open-ended questions allow students to express what's on their minds, and they pave the way for the teacher to pose additional questions, delve further, and bring out students' deeper thoughts. Open-ended questions begin with *what, how,* or *why,* question words that stimulate thought and creativity.

Row 1: Basic Questions

The first row on the Questions for Life Cue Words chart shows the Perception triangle. (See Figure 5.1 on page 51.) The triangle was chosen to signify individual instances of perception—tangible, concrete instances of *observing, feeling, tasting,* or perceiving in other ways that primarily involve the six senses. The circles that follow in Row 1 represent questioning strategies that create meaning from specific instances of perception. The three questioning strategies shown within the circles show distinct but related ways of thinking about the instances: "What *common characteristics* were found in those instances (Induction*)*? How would you *categorize* those instances (Analysis)? How are those instances *similar* to others you have experienced in the past? How are they *different* (Same/Different)?"

In our thinking, several instances—each represented by a triangle to provide a more concrete picture—combine to form, for example, a *generalization.* This process constitutes thinking inductively, represented by the circle in Figure 5.2 on page 52. The instances might also have led to a recognition of *patterns, qualities, rules,* or *common elements* or *characteristics.* All, however, are aspects of the thinking process called Induction. We are moving from parts (instances of Perception) to a whole (Induction).

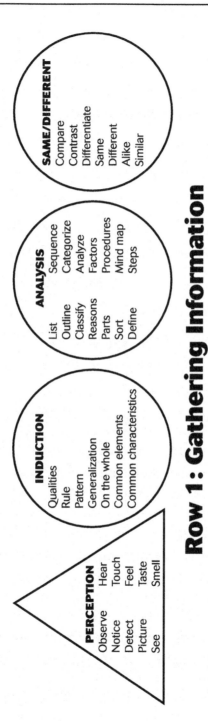

PERCEPTION

Observe
Notice
Detect
Picture
See
Hear
Touch
Feel
Taste
Smell

INDUCTION

Qualities
Rule
Pattern
Generalization
On the whole
Common elements
Common characteristics

ANALYSIS

List
Outline
Classify
Reasons
Parts
Sort
Define
Sequence
Categorize
Analyze
Factors
Procedures
Mind map
Steps

SAME/DIFFERENT

Compare
Contrast
Differentiate
Same
Different
Alike
Similar

Row 1: Gathering Information

Figure 5.1

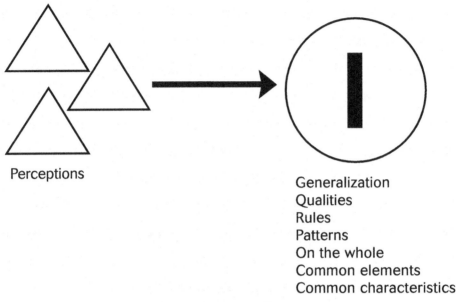

Perceptions

Generalization
Qualities
Rules
Patterns
On the whole
Common elements
Common characteristics

Induction

Figure 5.2

One might also start with the thought process of Induction—*generalizations, common characteristics, rules, qualities,* or *patterns*. From those we might look at what instances or perceptions led up to the Induction. The listing of these instances makes this process one of Analysis. Here we move from the whole (Induction in this case but, as we shall see later, from other thoughts processes as well) to individual parts. (See Figure 5.3 on page 53.)

An Analysis breaks down a whole into *parts, steps, reasons, lists,* etc. For example, you might explain to your students that all proper nouns begin with a capital letter. This is the rule, or whole. The students' task is to identify which words in a sentence are proper nouns needing capitalization. The sentence might be: "Nancy and lisa went to the sunrise mall," students would identify—list—"lisa" and "sunrise" and "mall" as words that need to be capitalized. Their response shows that they were using the critical thinking skill of Analysis.

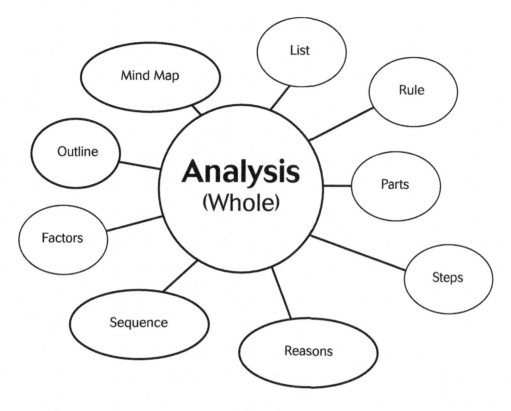

Figure 5.3

In another example, if students went on a field trip to a museum the field trip represents the whole. To break it down into parts, you might ask students to identify the sequence of what occurred (*sequencing* is the thinking skill of *analysis* too): first they took the bus, then they entered the museum; they explored five rooms; they had lunch; they returned to the bus; and they rode the bus back to school.

The various *parts, steps, reasons*, etc., we use in Analysis can also be augmented by comparing them to something *similar* or *different* (Same/Different), creating additional *parts, steps, reasons*, etc.

Just as we went from Perception to Induction, we can also go from Analysis to Induction, again from *parts* to a *whole*. For example, perhaps you go on a family vacation and on your return decide to *list* the highlights of your trip (Analysis). In doing so, you might come to see a *pattern* (Induction) in your journey, and you might make the *generalization* (Induction) that you spent too much time in the car and too little time in any of the nice places. In doing so, you might recall a prior trip that was the *same* because it was a family road trip, but was *different* because you spent more time seeing the sights and less time in the car (Same/Different) (See Figure 5.4)

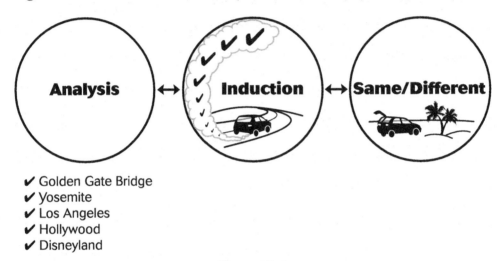

✔ Golden Gate Bridge
✔ Yosemite
✔ Los Angeles
✔ Hollywood
✔ Disneyland

Figure 5.4

This example demonstrates how naturally our brains go from one thought process to another. The three thinking processes Induction, Analysis, and Same/Different flow together and support one another.

Potluck: Perception, Induction, Analysis

Let's look at another example. You are back at school after taking some time off. You have conducted your morning classes and are now walking down the hall. You begin to smell something cooking, something that smells like pizza or pasta sauce. As you approach the faculty room, you hear people talking and laughing. You peek inside and see one of your colleagues stirring a large pot of something on the school's small stove. Other faculty members are placing dishes of food on a long table adjacent to the stove; some are stacking paper plates, forks, and napkins.

The smell is definitely pasta sauce! Your stomach starts to growl and you realize you are hungry. As you walk into the room, your colleagues welcome you with their smiles and gestures.

From all of these perceived instances, you recognize a *pattern* containing all the *common characteristics* of every faculty potluck you have attended in the past. (See Figure 5.5)

Now let's say instead that you return from your time off and are approached by one of your colleagues. He informs you that the new administrator has noticed that teachers frown frequently, speak in clipped sentences, move rapidly down the hallways, and avoid making eye contact. Basing his opinion on these observations (Perception), the administrator has made the *generalization* that his staff appears stressed. He has scheduled a luncheon get-together as a way to relieve stress, do some team building, and improve morale. Your colleague says the administrator offered to make his famous pasta sauce for this lunch if others would chip in and set up a potluck. Your colleague agreed to organize one and is now asking for your help.

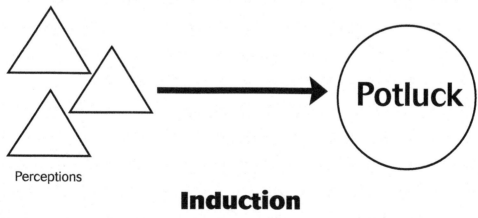

Perceptions

Induction

Figure 5.5

Here you have the administrator making a *generalization,* which in this case takes the form of a response to *observations*: staff is stressed. He decides to hold a fun event in the form of a potluck to help relieve this stress.

You and your colleague begin *listing* what *steps* you will need to take (the parts you must include) to implement the potluck. (See Figure 5.6) You also need to *sort* the *steps* into a logical *sequence.* In short, you must do an Analysis. In this situation the potluck is the *generalization,* and you are *analyzing* its *parts* by breaking them down into a *list* and arranging them in a *sequence*

- Announce the event.
- Determine who will attend.
- Assign dishes for various faculty members to bring.
- Gather plates, utensils, and napkins.

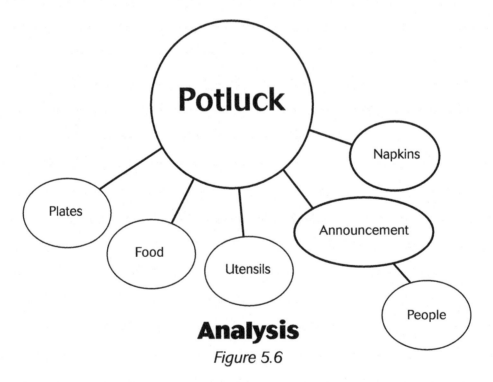

Analysis

Figure 5.6

Classroom: Induction, Analysis

Here is another example: In a classroom an educator asked her students to read a paragraph in which all the nouns were underlined. She told the students that she would be asking them to come up with a definition for the word *noun* after they had read and studied the words. She was asking them to use the thinking skill Induction—to look at examples of nouns and develop a *generalization* about the meaning (to look at the individual parts and come up with the *whole*). (See Figure 5.7)

The qualities of a noun are: _____
(Write a definition.)

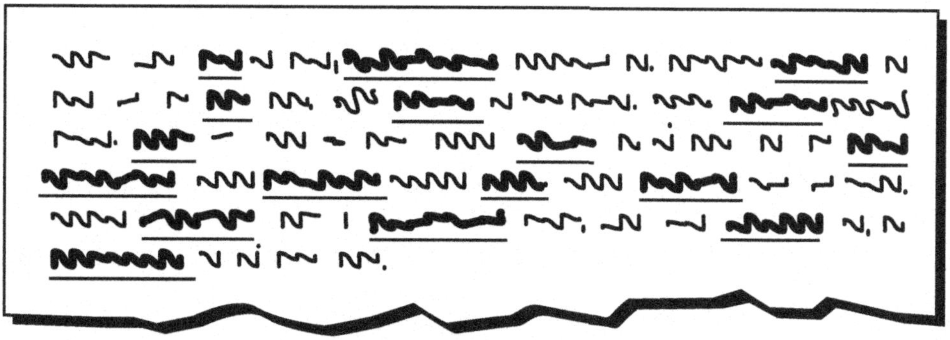

Induction
Figure 5.7

The next day she asked her students to read the definition of *noun* and discuss it. Then she gave them a paragraph and asked them to underline all the nouns. This was Analysis: students understood the *whole* and then listed its *parts*. (See Figure 5.8 on page 58.)

A noun is a part of speech that names a person, place, thing, or idea.
Underline all nouns.

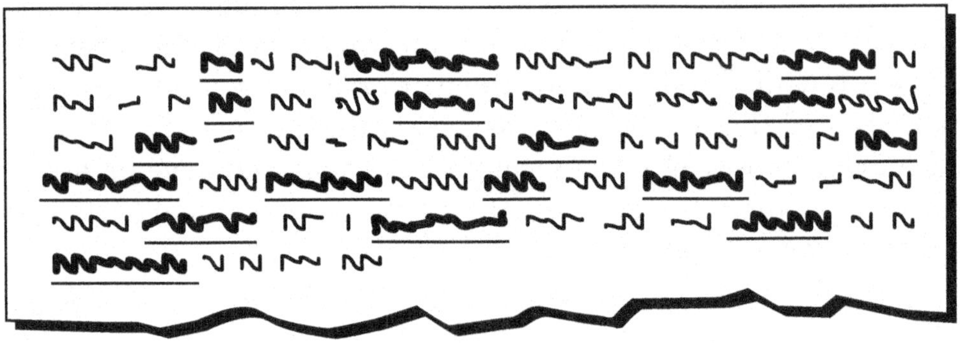

Analysis
Figure 5.8

Rows 2 and 3: Complex Questions

Row 2 of the Questions for Life Cue Words chart begins with the critical thinking skill called Insight. (See Figure 5.9 on page 59.) Insight represents a form of advanced Induction; we might say it is Induction to the second power. Because it goes beyond basic Induction, on the chart it is represented as being "in the clouds" (hence the shape). An *insight* in the potluck example might be that the new administrator is very aware of staff morale. In the example of students working on nouns, the teacher's *insight* might be that her students were more creative when they used Induction to define *noun*.

Just as the thought processes in Row 1 are similar and move naturally from one to another, Appraisal, Summary, and Evaluation inside the rectangles in Row 2 lead from one to another in a natural mind progression. Summary and Evaluation often depend on Appraisal. For example, after the potluck the administrator might want to *appraise* how the event accomplished its goal:

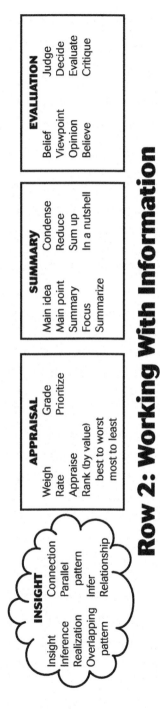

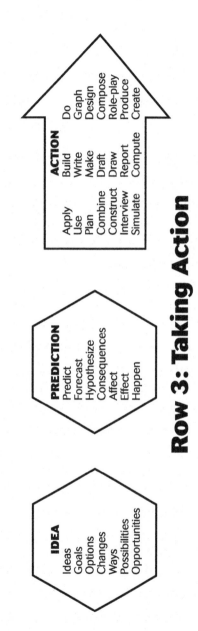

INSIGHT

Insight	Connection
Inference	Parallel
Realization	pattern
Overlapping	Infer
pattern	Relationship

APPRAISAL

Weigh	Grade
Rate	Prioritize
Appraise	
Rank (by value)	
best to worst	
most to least	

SUMMARY

Main idea	Condense
Main point	Reduce
Summary	Sum up
Focus	In a nutshell
Summarize	

EVALUATION

Belief	Judge
Viewpoint	Decide
Opinion	Evaluate
Believe	Critique

Row 2: Working With Information

IDEA

Ideas
Goals
Options
Changes
Ways
Possibilities
Opportunities

PREDICTION

Predict
Forecast
Hypothesize
Consequences
Affect
Effect
Happen

ACTION

Apply	Do
Use	Graph
Plan	Design
Combine	Compose
Construct	Role-play
Interview	Produce
Simulate	Create
	Build
	Write
	Make
	Draft
	Draw
	Report
	Compute

Row 3: Taking Action

Figure 5.9

"How would staff *rate* the potluck on a scale of 1 through 10?" Then he might *summarize* what took place and/or *evaluate* the results in terms of morale building. The teacher in the classroom might *weigh* (Appraise) which way of learning about nouns seemed to engage her students most and *summarize* the success or challenges of the lessons when meeting with her coach. From this, she might *decide* whether to repeat the activity for another part of speech (Evaluation).

In Row 3 the hexagons containing Idea and Prediction represent the times we synthesize in order to arrive at Action, shown inside the broad arrow shape. The classroom teacher came up with the *idea* of teaching nouns in two ways, questioned herself as to what might *happen* if she did so (Prediction), and then went ahead with the exercise (Action).

While making major decisions or problem solving around important issues often works best when we begin with Row 1 and move through to Action in Row 3, the individual Questions for Life questioning strategies do *not* have to be used sequentially as shown on the chart. We can easily start with an initial *action* and then go back to gather information to take the *action* further; or after completing the *action,* we can *analyze* what happened. Or we can *predict* and then *observe* (Perception), *appraise, evaluate,* or otherwise work with information to see how close the *prediction* came to reality. Our minds are capable of moving around the Questions for Life chart rapidly in many different patterns.

The point is to identify and become aware of the kind of thinking the brain is engaged in, regardless of the path taken through the thinking processes. You may not need to sit down and diagram your thinking process in every situation, but understanding the process for making complex decisions, solving problems, or dealing with challenging circumstances helps to streamline thinking and make it more effective.

The Integration of Thinking Processes

As mentioned earlier, Questions for Life was initially developed to help teachers improve their questioning strategies and recognize that the same thinking processes apply to all types of curriculums. You will recall, for example, that educators who applied a certain type of critical thinking to reading comprehension strategies did not realize that the same type of thinking applied also to classroom management strategies (that they might be *analyzing, predicting,* or *evaluating* in both cases). We call this the integration of thinking processes. Once the teachers identified a common vocabulary, thinking processes became clear and the cue words that invoke them could be readily applied.

From there it is a short step to realizing that students usually don't see the integration of thinking processes either. They, too, lack a vehicle for making a connection between Analysis in literature, for example, and Analysis in science. In addition, they seldom make a connection between the shrewd thinking strategies they use outside of school and the thinking strategies they need to apply in school. They don't connect their *analysis* of the features of a particular Web site, for example, with the *analysis* they are asked to make of the components of a story or a science experiment.

It really boils down to awareness: the more students—or educators or others—become aware of the types of thinking required to formulate an opinion, make a decision, solve a problem, create a plan, etc., the better they are able to achieve successful results. Certainly we all know how to think, but identifying the process, being aware of exactly how we develop thought into *action,* greatly boosts our success. No one is suggesting that we always stop and *analyze* every aspect of our thinking, but the Questions for Life model offers a great tool for thinking awareness.

We can't apply tools, however, when we haven't identified their function.

Ready, Set, Go!
The Three Rows of Questions for Life

The questioning strategies in the first row focus on gathering data or information. As the information is collected, it may be *analyzed* and/or *compared* or *contrasted* to other data for better understanding. A *generalization* may then be formed. Some or all of these thinking processes might occur, but using any of the thinking in the first row always involves gathering information or data in one way or another:

"What flavors do you *taste* in this cookie?"

"What are *common characteristics* of Generation X?"

"What *procedures* should be followed to solve this type of problem?"

"*Compare* the two frogs' hind legs."

The second row involves thinking strategies that work with information, whether gathered by using the thinking processes in the first row or already available from prior experience or knowledge. We can work with the information by using the cue words in each questioning type:

"What *insights* do we get from the report provided?"

"How would you *rank* the suggestions people submitted in the report?"

"*Summarize* the *main idea* presented."

"What do you *believe* about it?"

In the second row we look to see if we want to gather more information or move to Action—in other words, move back to Row 1 or go on to Row 3. We decide if there is a reason to *do* something now that we have collected and worked with the information.

The third row is driven by new thoughts and *action,* usually stemming from the information and thinking that prevailed in Rows 1 and 2. *Action* is physical and requires *doing, building, drawing, graphing,* etc. Its chances of success are greater when the thought processes in Row 3 have come into play: when new *ideas* have been *created* out of gathered information and when *predictions* have been made. Questions the thought processes in Row 3 might address include:

"What are some *ways* we might approach creating a model?"

"What do you think will *happen* when we use each of these approaches?"

"Can you *construct* a model based on our prior planning and research?"

Education Concentrates on Rows 1 and 2

Much of teaching operates using only the skills in the first and second rows of the Questions for Life model. Lessons tend to focus on gathering and working with data without employing the important skills of taking *action,* making *predictions,* or developing new *ideas.* This stems not from educators' or students' inability to use those skills, but from education's focus on amassing large amounts of knowledge, working with it, and then moving on to the next chapter, the next textbook, or the next standard without offering permission, time, or facility to apply thinking directly to *action.*

Summarizing a book in a report does not constitute the type of critical thinking represented in Row 3 because it is not proactive—it is manipulating information already obtained. *Evaluating* also entails developing a *belief* or an *opinion* based on already existing information. *Believing, deciding,* or having an *opinion* about something has the potential to lead to the next logical step of *doing* something, yet that step is rarely taken.

Of course, many good thinking skills are represented by the processes in Rows 1 and 2. They are the basis for higher-level thinking. The real purpose of using complex critical thinking skills in education, however, is to take *action,* as happens in life, in which we actually do something as a result of our thinking. Thinking much and doing nothing is ultimately a waste of time.

Taking Action in a Vacuum

The obverse is also true: many of us take *action* without first scrutinizing data or information relevant to that *action*.

In his book *Straight Talk: Turning Communication Upside Down for Strategic Results at Work,* author and management consultant Eric F. Douglas provides a model he calls the "Circle of Assumptions."[1] In the center of the circle is the word *Data;* subsequent rings moving out from the center are labeled *Interpretation, Evaluation, Conclusion,* and *Action.* Douglas shows how we often draw conclusions or take action without first collecting data or (if we did collect it) questioning its validity. The action or conclusion is taken or accepted blindly, particularly if there's a person behind it with a strong communication style. Douglas cites an example of a common failure in critical thinking: using an evaluation based on an assumption to support a conclusion or action. "This is like building a house on sand," he states.

Similarly, educators or administrators might go directly to taking *action* without *analyzing, appraising, summarizing,* or *evaluating* information about how and why to take the *action*. They might fail to ask pertinent questions about what might be included in the *action,* what might be discarded, what other *ideas* might work better, or what *predictions* might be made for its success.

For example, a teacher who simply asks students to "create a science project for the upcoming science fair" is requesting *action* with so little accompanying information that students may not know how to start thinking about the project. Faculty or committee members, administrators, state mandates, or public officials might initiate a program—an *action*—but fail to explain what it entails or why they are requiring it.

In their book *Building Teachers' Capacity for Success,* Pete Hall and Alisa Simeral discuss how problems can occur when schools initiate "programs" for school improvement. They quote educational researcher and writer Michael Fullan, who says:

> People should be seeking ideas that help them develop their own thinking rather than programs. . . . Teachers suppress their creative intellect and ignore their prior training in order to follow a lockstep, one-size-fits-all instructional program.[2]

Summary

The thinking processes in all three rows of the Questions for Life model flow from one to another, often simultaneously. To develop clarity when tackling issues and problems, it is highly useful to employ the thinking involved one row at a time, to become familiar with and practice questioning strategies, and then to develop and understand a game plan. To this end, we begin in the next chapter to consider each row individually, commencing with Questions for Life Row 1: Gathering the Data.

Chapter 6
Gathering the Data
QFL Row 1

Row 1: Finding Solutions

There was a time not very long ago when people used to fix things that were broken. Imagine that! If a gadget, appliance, or tool wasn't functioning, we would take it apart to find out what was wrong. If we were smart, we'd lay the pieces out sequentially—perhaps number them—to make sure we could put them back together again once we fixed what was wrong. We looked carefully at each part, picking it up and handling it, feeling for scratches or other defects. We observed the whole and noticed each individual part.

If there was a functioning part in the gadget similar to the one not working, we would look to see how they were the same and how they were different. We would make an analysis of the working and nonworking parts so we could figure out, or generalize, from what we found whether we could fix the gadget or whether it was beyond repair, and it was time, after all, to buy another.

All of that thinking is represented in Row 1 of the Questions for Life model: we *touched* and *observed* the part (Perception); we *compared* parts that were working with those that were not (Same/Different); we *analyzed* and *categorized* the various *parts* (Analysis) and then made a *generalization* based on what we *observed* and what we knew from past experiences (Induction). (See Figure 6.1 on page 69.)

In our throw-away society, in which technology creates ever more products at ever cheaper prices, fixing things may have gone to the landfill along with our malfunctioning possessions. Technology today has taken a lot of responsibility away from us. It sometimes even has us using public restrooms without having to think about flushing the toilet or turning on the water at the sink. If one faucet doesn't work, we move to the next, never thinking that there is a way to fix the broken one.

Likewise, too often when students face problems or decisions, they look to others for solutions or direction. Just as we move to the next faucet, they "go on the Internet"—education's modern mantra.

Simply going through the thinking required in the first row of the Questions for Life model would give students—or adults—the freedom to solve (fix) their own problems and come up with their own decisions. And the operative word here is *freedom*—freedom for students to think for themselves creatively and confidently.

Perception

The first row of the Questions for Life model comprises the most basic thinking skills. Perception probably has a harder time than the other thinking processes. (See Figure 6.2 on page 70.) As we plow ahead to decide, act, or analyze, we forget to *observe* and *hear* what's right in front of us—to *smell* the roses, if you will—so we can really *see* what we're dealing with. Our perceptions are the raw data at the center of Douglas' Circle of Assumptions mentioned in Chapter 5.

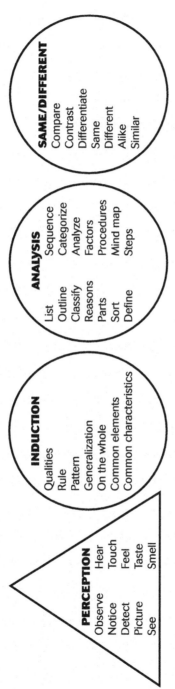

PERCEPTION

Observe	Hear
Notice	Touch
Detect	Feel
Picture	Taste
See	Smell

INDUCTION

Qualities
Rule
Pattern
Generalization
On the whole
Common elements
Common characteristics

ANALYSIS

List	Sequence
Outline	Categorize
Classify	Analyze
Reasons	Factors
Parts	Procedures
Sort	Mind map
Define	Steps

SAME/DIFFERENT

Compare
Contrast
Differentiate
Same
Different
Alike
Similar

Row 1: Gathering Information

Figure 6.1

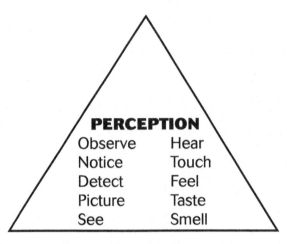

Figure 6.2

The cue words under Perception on the Questions for Life Cue Words chart focus our thinking on the concrete, the observable, and the literal. Being very clear about what we *see, hear, smell, feel, touch, detect,* and so on prevents us from making wrong assumptions based on a lack of concrete facts. With Perception, what we *see* is what we get, and what we do with what we *see* stems from the experience of our own senses. In the classroom or in any group, relying on observable data puts everyone on the same page.

We use our multisensory perception all the time, of course, and it often serves as the starting point for making decisions. If we are going to purchase a cell phone, for example, our first inclination is to *observe, touch, hear,* or *picture* it for ourselves. Perhaps we take a look at our colleague's Blackberry, play with the keyboard or touchpad, and try out each feature. We hold it in our hand, *feel* its grip, and *notice* how smooth it is.

We might *compare* it (Same/Different) with another one we are considering. Here again, our Perception would kick in as we *observed, noticed,* and *touched* each one. We would make an *analysis* of the features of each, *listing* them mentally or on paper. We'd *compare* the price against the features (Same/Different), and then add these *factors* to our *list* (Analysis). We might then come to the *generalization* that the Blackberry devices we are considering have *common characteristics* (Induction), but that, *on the whole,* we like the first one we looked at best (Evaluation). All of these decisions start with Perception.

During this process, of course, we are not necessarily consciously asking ourselves the questions associated with each thought process, but we are going through them nevertheless. As educators, we can see how probing with cue words, such as those in our Blackberry example, might direct our own thought processes and those of our students toward the kind of thinking we were seeking: Do we need to *analyze?* Do they need to stop and *observe* (Perception)? Is it time for a *comparison* (Same/Different)?

Perception often gets overlooked in the classroom because we assume everyone *saw* or *felt* what we did. When we refer to something, we imagine everyone has had the same prior experience. For example, if we start asking questions about the ocean and there are students in the class who have never *seen, touched,* or *heard* an ocean, we have made an assumption that will immediately leave those students out of the ensuing thinking processes. Unless everyone recognizes the same or similar sensations (*hear, see, touch, feel,* etc.), the natural thought processes get derailed.

To engage the students who have never experienced an ocean, we need to provide them with some tangible items from the ocean to hold and *observe*—perhaps show them a movie about the ocean or give them a shell that still has the scent of saltwater. We could also do a mental imaging, or visualization, about what an ocean looks like, sounds like, and smells like. In this way students who would otherwise be "ocean-challenged" could acquire multisensory experiences similar to those of the other students. Sharing common perceptions, students could then move along the first row of questioning strategies together.

Paying careful attention to Perception also allows us to shift our focus from how we see things to how others might see them. For example, a teacher *hears* two students speaking loudly on the other side of the room and *sees* their bodies looking tense and agitated. The teacher makes an assumption—a form of Induction—and calls out to discipline them for acting out. But what exactly did the teacher *see, hear,* and *notice* that led to that assumption? Loud talking and agitated behavior. Yet the students might have *seen* themselves as people in a heated discussion, perhaps having a good argument over something the teacher had assigned. They did not *notice* they were speaking loudly; they thought they were having a conversation.

The teacher and students had different perceptions, which caused their inductive reasoning to differ also. They made assumptions without using any Analysis to test them out. How often do we get caught by assuming someone *saw* or *heard* what we *saw* and *heard?* Simply asking in the future, "What did you *observe?*" could clear up a lot of embarrassment in our lives!

Rather than starting with assumptions or inductive thinking, teachers can benefit by asking themselves about their own perceptions:

> "What body language do I *observe* the students exhibiting during this activity?"

> "What intonation did I *hear* in the students' answers when I asked them to move down the hall?"

> "What do I *hear* students say that I can paraphrase back?"

> "What do I *notice* about students' behavior toward one another so that I can better understand them?"

Concrete, literal data falls in the realm of Perception, and the more we endeavor to start there, focusing on our perceptions, the more astute our assumptions and actions will be.

Importance of Student Perception

When students hold a concrete object, such as an apple, they gain a greater knowledge about the object than when they are shown a picture of it. Give students an apple and ask them to describe it: "What do you *see?* How does the skin *feel?* What does it *smell* like? *Notice* the stem. What does it sound like when you bite into it? And what is the *taste?* Can you describe it?"

Now hand students an orange. "What do you *see? Touch* the orange and push into the skin. How does it *feel?* Can you *smell* it? Now pull off the skin. What does that *feel* like on your fingers? Can you *smell* it? What does it *taste* like?"

Of course, the thinking that immediately follows Perception in a case like this is Same/Different, rendering the common expression "comparing apples to oranges" something your students will remember for life.

Let's take another example. In a chemistry class a teacher might ask students to look into a microscope. "What do you *see?*" Since an actual physical description is not usually what teachers want, students will struggle to recall what this thing they are looking at is called. "Amoeba . . . ?" replies one student timidly. Wanting to elicit perceptions involving the senses rather than accept a label, the teacher asks again, "What do you *see?* What do you *notice* about its shape?" These are the questions that, taken literally, will elicit Perception. Answers that give a name or label instead of literally stating what is *seen, smelled, felt,* or *heard* move to Induction, jumping past Perception.

Maybe the chemistry teacher hands out another slide and asks students to once again *notice* what they *see,* and describe what it looks like, sounds like, etc. Once Perception is established, the teacher may request that students identify and write down the *common characteristics* they observe, moving them to Induction and then to a *comparison* (Same/Different). This is a natural thinking progression involving all the skills in Row 1.

All of these steps lead to a better understanding of the subject and provide room for more discussion. We can readily see that this process of learning far exceeds the deductive process of having students name or label items from their own system of recall, which may have nothing to do with the nature of what they are observing.

Visualization and Mindfulness: Aids to Perception

In the absence of actual physical data teachers may trigger the thought process Perception using guided imagery or visualization. This process enables them to guide their students by "painting a picture" of a scene or object so that each student can perceive or experience it individually.

To counteract the anxiety many students feel in school because of stressful home situations, poverty, excessive testing, or peer pressure, an elementary school in Oakland, California, introduced a program called "Mindful Schools," which introduces students to the practice of mindfulness, a form of meditation.[1] For 15 minutes a day, three times a week, students sit quietly with their eyes closed, breathing deeply and rhythmically. They focus on particular sensations as they are asked to *touch* and *smell* a raisin or some other piece of food before *tasting* it, or to *notice, observe,* and *hear* the sounds in the room. Mindfulness is achieved when students become aware of what is happening in the present moment without judgment.

Using their perceptions in this way, they are able to calm down and pay attention. They stop and take a moment to consciously *notice,* which is key to using Perception. As a result, teachers have begun to see less stress and anger and far less bullying. Students are able to concentrate when they are told to stop and *notice,* and they are able to take a deep breath, which also triggers the state of mindfulness.

Induction

As we noted earlier, the thinking skills Induction, Analysis, and Same/Different are placed within the same geometrical shape in the Questions for Life model because they are often used simultaneously or in sequence. We are moving to Induction here for purposes of explanation only; thought processes do not follow an established order. (See Figure 6.3) Our thought processes could—and usually do—move all around the Questions for Life Cue Words chart.

Induction is the process of making a *generalization* or an assumption that is drawn from instances or experiences. As shown in Figure 6.3, Induction allows us to find *common characteristics* among multiple instances and discern a *pattern* or create a *rule* that applies to them all.

When we use Induction, however, our *generalizations* and assumptions can be wrong, as in the case of the teacher in our earlier example who assumed that her students were quarreling. There is no "right" *generalization* or inductive answer, precisely because it is based on our own experiences, our own instances, and our own

Figure 6.3

perceptions. We can, of course, add the experiences and instances of others to the mix, and doing so often improves our chances of arriving at a more accurate *generalization.* The more instances we have, and the more we scrutinize what we saw, heard, or felt in those instances, the more likely we are to arrive at a valid *generalization, rule,* or *pattern.* Such scrutiny helps to eliminate wrong thinking based on guesswork or misinformation. Still, though, the end result of inductive thinking comes from within, from our own personal thought processes (unlike deductive thinking, in which we are given information presented from outside ourselves).

This propensity of inductive thinking to produce mistaken *generalizations* may be illustrated by a story about a young second grader who shared with his teacher that Jesus Christ was a dog. The teacher was taken aback and asked the boy how he ever came to think that.

"I learned it in Sunday school," the boy replied proudly. "Jesus is a dog, and I even know what kind!"

"What kind would that be?" asked the teacher.

"A shepherd! He's a shepherd who takes care of the sheep when they run away—like a German Shepherd," he declared.

The child's picture of what a shepherd is and the instance of hearing his Sunday school teacher talk about Christ as a shepherd led the boy to a false assumption based on inductive thinking. A few Perception questions by the teacher could have helped him out!

Induction Cue Words

A beginning teacher receives a warm welcome from her colleagues; she is assigned a caring mentor who walks her through the school's procedures and culture; her classroom is cheerful, roomy, and relatively new. When this new teacher's friend asks, "So, *on the whole,* what can you conclude about your new school?" the question and its cue words point her thinking toward the *qualities* and *patterns* she observed and lead her to respond, "My school is a warm and friendly place."

In the same way, when working with students, a teacher would ask a question or make a statement using the cue words that elicit the thinking process the teacher seeks. To solicit Induction, then, the teacher would use the cue words *qualities, rule, pattern, generalization, on the whole, common characteristics,* and *common elements.*

For example, a teacher using Induction cue words might ask a primary student:

> "What are some *common characteristics* of puppies?"

> "From your visit to the retirement home, what are some of the *qualities* of older people?"

Elementary teachers talking to older children might ask:

> "*On the whole,* what can you say about situations where mom is the only parent in the home?"

> "What do these three words have in *common?*"

> "What was the *common element* in the three problems?"

And middle school:

> "In our simulation of the stock market, what *patterns* did you see when people bought and sold stock?"

> "After reviewing all the facts in the documentary, make a *generalization* about diet and exercise."

And in high school or postsecondary:

"What are the *common characteristics* of the secondary characters in the story?"

"What *pattern* is there in this sequence of numbers?"

"What *common elements* are shared by governments we have studied—democracy, dictatorship, and republic?"

Analysis and Same/Different

We often do an *analysis* or a *comparison* (Same/Different) before or after we arrive at a *generalization*. We can also perform these processes simultaneously. (See Figure 6.4) Every solution-seeking and thinking process has Analysis questions at its center. Analysis questions allow us to break an issue apart and look at its *parts* individually in order to gain a better understanding of all the nuances

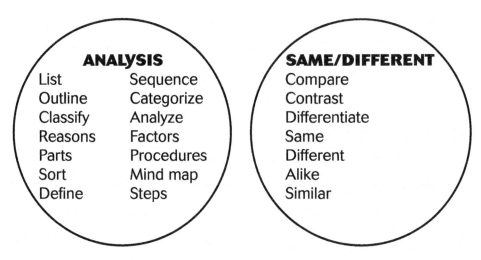

Figure 6.4

involved. We can even *analyze* the questioning strategies we might use, *sequencing* them in our heads and *listing* the cue words we will use to produce the thinking process we seek. Our brains naturally *compare* and *contrast* information during Analysis, and each *analysis* becomes richer and more in-depth as we determine *similarities* and *differences* among the individual elements we are considering. The *comparison* brings forth more details about each one, providing greater clarity and understanding.

Analyses can be developed in countless different ways. Analysis appears in formats such as *outlines, mind maps, classifications, lists,* and *categories.* Drop-down menus on computer programs are *analyses* showing *lists* of options within each menu. Students can be asked to *sort,* give *reasons, list factors,* make a *mind map, outline,* or describe the *steps* or *sequence* of a process. All of these cue words lead to Analysis. (See Figure 6.5 on page 80 for a depiction of five types of Analysis.)

Where Perception or Induction questions might ask for a specific observation or generalization, Analysis questions ask for multiple perceptions or generalizations. Same/Different questions augment the Analysis.

Row 1: Your Friends

Here's an exercise that illustrates how the thinking processes work together. Take a piece of paper and draw a line down the middle, creating two columns, A and B. Close your eyes and visualize one of your good friends standing before you. Visualize this person both close up and from afar, viewing the whole body. Recall conversations you have had with this person, including some of the specific things he or she may have said to you. Recreate the feelings you have about your friend.

Now open your eyes and at the top of the left-hand column, column A, write the person's name and then list his or her physical

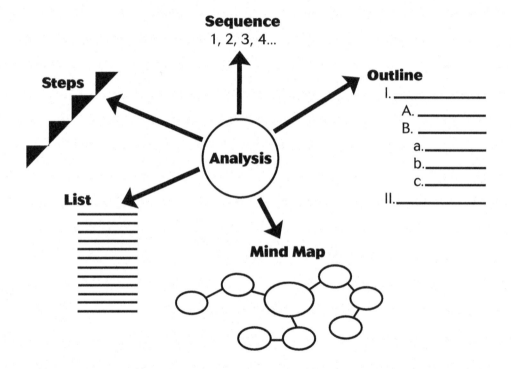

Figure 6.5

attributes, such as "tall" or "stocky." Add some of the person's personality traits, such as "shy" or "caring."

Close your eyes again and picture another friend. Concentrate on this friend for a moment, recalling conversations and what he or she looks like. Open your eyes and write this person's name at the top of column B. List a few of his or her physical attributes and personality traits. As you make this second list, you may find you want to borrow some words you have written in column A and add them to column B, or that you listed some qualities in column B that should also be in column A. Feel free to add to and borrow from each list.

When you are finished, you will note that this exercise encompassed all the thinking processes identified in Row 1 of Questions for Life. What you visualized was Perception, a sensory recall of what you *saw, heard,* and *felt.* When you recalled various personality traits of each person, you placed *meaning* on your perceptions and immediately moved into the realm of Induction—you thought of *patterns* and *qualities* as you made lists. You were making *generalizations* based on instances of your friends' behaviors.

This becomes important when we try to make correct decisions based on facts and raw data rather than on the meaning we create from that data. In forensics, for example, a crime scene investigator works to establish facts without prematurely assigning meaning to them or speculating about how the crime was committed. Doing so helps to keep the investigation honest, accurate, and open to all possibilities.

When you listed the personality traits of your friends, noting combinations of characteristics that were meaningful to you, your brain engaged automatically in Same/Different thinking by making *comparisons*. For example, if you chose the word *funny* for one of your friends, your brain automatically considered and rejected comparisons with words like *serious* or *boring*. This *listing* and *sorting* comprises the thinking process Analysis, which was augmented in our exercise when you *compared* your two friends and added to your *lists* as you determined what was the *same* and what was *different* about them.

Scenario of the Future

Within our minds we can freely visualize what we know and what we want to see. As societies, we can create visions for the future. Just as Perception questions may start a process that leads to Action, so, too, does perceiving in the mind's eye create future actions.

Let's apply this visualization process to a classroom or school scenario. Picture your ideal classroom or school of the future—a future that begins tomorrow or three months or a year from this moment. What physical things are present? What do you *see?* What do you *hear?* Is it bright? High tech? Who is there? What are they doing? How is this classroom the *same* as the one you currently have or others you have seen? What are the *common patterns?* What *differences* do you see? What *qualities* are there? *On the whole,* how would these changes affect your teaching?

Once you have visualized them, *list* the aspects you would want to have in a future classroom or school. What *reasons* might you have for wanting them? *Outline* your purposes for creating such a classroom or school. Perhaps you can create a *mind map* similar to the one shown in Figure 6.5 on page 80.

Drawing on the data you generate from asking yourself these questions, you might want to conduct an activity along similar lines with your students. Use cue words to ask them to visualize (Perception) an ideal classroom of the future. Ask them to *list* the *reasons* why they think this classroom is ideal. Ask them to *outline* the *factors* or *steps* involved in creating it. See if they can share how it is *similar* to and how it is *different* from the existing classroom or school.

Pair students up and have them share the *qualities* they developed for their classrooms of the future, noting *common characteristics* or *patterns*. Have the students *compare* their two visions and add to their *lists*. Then repeat the inductive exercise of determining the *common elements* of each.

All of this work gathering data or information is occurring in Row 1. By combining your visions, *analyses*, and *generalizations* with those of your students and seeing the many ways in which your gathered information is connected, you and your students may well come up with some important insights about the classroom or school of the future.

So now, quite naturally, we will move to Insight and the other thought processes on Row 2 of Questions for Life.

Chapter 7
Making Do With
What You've Got
QFL Row 2

If you ever wonder where the twin demons procrastination and indecision live, wonder no more—they're in Row 1 of Questions for Life. In Row 1 we gather information, but if we don't work with it, no decision or action will ever take place. If we confine our thinking exclusively to the processes in Row 1, we will simply collect data, note its characteristics, gather more data, compare it to what we had before, notice some more, gather some more, analyze some more—we've been over this before! The phrase "analysis paralysis" comes to mind.

The basic thinking skills in Row 1 are the heart and soul of the future, more complex thinking that is found in Rows 2 and 3. Without a foundation of information—*observations, patterns, lists, comparisons,* etc.—we would be unable to achieve *insights* and we would have nothing to *act* upon. Row 1 serves not only as the foundation for the Questions for Life thinking processes that follow but also as a place to return to once *ideas* have been generated or *action* has been taken at the end of Row 3. The process is circular because taking action so often results in the need to gather new data to make another decision, solve another problem, or take yet another action.

Insight

Because our brains will go wherever our thinking processes naturally take them, using Questions for Life cue words to gather information and perceive what is right in front of us leads us to the *insights* that begin Row 2. (See Figure 7.1 on page 87.) Remember: Insight can be thought of as Induction to the second power—Induction on steroids, if you will. The thinking process Induction involves capturing various instances that we perceived or analyzed (what we saw, noticed, felt, heard, compared, sorted, etc.) and coming to an assumption or generalization about them, perhaps detecting a certain pattern. Insight, going a step beyond Induction, captures several such generalizations and creates an "aha" moment—an *insight* about their *overlapping* or *parallel patterns,* as shown in Figure 7.2.

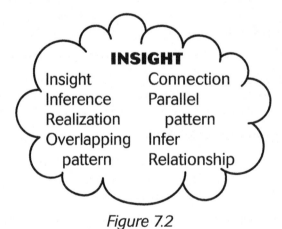

Figure 7.2

Row 2: Working With Information

Figure 7.1

Insight can be compared to a good soup. After all the ingredients are put into a pot and stirred, their flavors blend—and voila! Soup! We now have something altogether different that incorporates its individual ingredients but transforms them. And to carry our simile one step further, perhaps the steam rising from the soup can be compared to a cloud like the one representing Insight on the Questions for Life chart.

Insights vary in quality from very simple to highly complex. They are formed from associations not specifically connected to the topic at hand (as if they came out of the vapors). Such associations might develop from prior perceptions and experiences that led to earlier generalizations derived from inductive thinking. Applying these generalizations to new situations often creates Insight.

For example, looking for the moral of a story often invokes Insight. To understand the moral, we have to make a *connection* between what happened in the story and some aspect of real life. Insight lives in the worlds of symbolism, metaphor, allegory, parable, moral, analogy, fable, legend, and myth, all of which provide wonderful opportunities to teach students how to access Insight.

Insight also occurs in the classroom when debriefing a lesson, reading or discussing a book, or experiencing an event. Using the cue words shown below in italics, a teacher might elicit Insight from young students by asking questions like the following:

"What *realization* do you have about life as a firefighter?"

"What *connection* can you make between the story and your life at home?"

"Now that we have studied animals on the endangered species list, what *realization* comes to mind?"

And for middle, secondary, or postsecondary students:

"What *inference* can you draw about plant growth in our laboratory and plants growing in the shade outside?"

"What *connection* can you make between erosion and riding your bike off a marked trail?"

"What *parallel pattern* exists between the symbolism in the story and divorce?"

"What *insights* did you have about drugs after hearing Michael's speech about his experiences?"

Insight Through Reflection

If we have spent sufficient time with the questioning strategies in Row 1, Insight often occurs without any prompting. Before they are asked, students may excitedly raise their hands and share new thoughts and *insights* just because they are inspired by the data gathered from Row 1 questions. While listing the physical characteristics and personality traits of your two friends, as we did in Chapter 6, you might have had an *insight* about them—they both make you laugh, or perhaps you *realized* they are complete opposites. Your *realization,* which occurred without any prompting or questioning, constitutes Insight.

Insight also stems from taking the time to reflect, and that requires stepping back to stop, look, listen, and allow *insights* and *realizations* to come forth. While this may seem difficult, or as a teacher you may think you have no time for it, allowing reflection actually saves valuable time in the long run because of the significance of the *insights* brought forth. Having *insights* signifies that we have internalized what we have *noticed, analyzed,* and perhaps solved or *decided* upon. As we internalize, we become more capable of repeating a pattern, solving a problem again, or making a similar decision in the future.

Insights are also internalized in the act of journal writing. Like clouds, they can often float by, but writing them down anchors them in memory. Even five minutes of reflection combined with sharing or committing to paper the resulting *insights* can elevate the meaning of a lesson or learning substantially.

Beyond that, *insights* add a richer, more holistic and human approach to teaching. So much of education exists in the realm of Analysis—most textbooks consist almost entirely of analytical writing. Induction and its cousin Insight are prompted by teachers who help students recognize these thinking processes when they occur. In recognizing them, students learn to notice and look back on their experiences, come to their own *realizations,* draw their own *inferences,* and discover their own *connections*.

Appraisal and Evaluation

The three other thinking processes in Row 2 are shown in identical rectangular shapes because they, like the three circled processes in Row 1, represent thinking that can occur simultaneously.

We can *appraise* something at lightning speed—let's say, a list of available movies at the cinema or online. We *prioritize* or *rank* them according to some criterion: length, actors, theatre location, or genre. But even as we do that, we immediately and simultaneously *judge* them against our own *viewpoint* or values, *evaluating* them according to our beliefs or opinions.

Confusing Appraisal and Evaluation

It often happens that we confuse Appraisal and Evaluation, thinking we are using one when in fact we are using the other. (See Figure 7.3 on page 91.) In many cases an educator will ask an Appraisal question and the student will answer with an *evaluation*. The teacher may call the answer wrong, since it was based on *opinion* and the student did not respond with an *appraisal*.

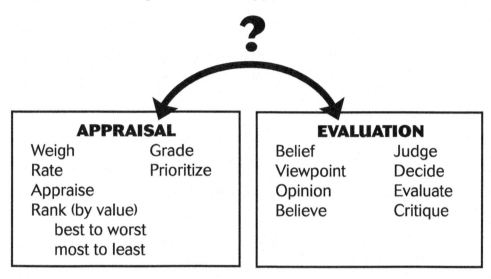

Figure 7.3

A teacher might ask, for example, "Which characters in the story had the *most* influence on the outcome and which ones had the *least?*"—an Appraisal question asking students to *rank* the characters' influence, most to least. If a student heard the inquiry as an Evaluation question, he or she might answer, "Well, I thought Frank was the most powerful because he kept the others from being captured." This is an Evaluation answer based on the student's value for protection or *belief* about Frank's motives.

The answer was correct for Evaluation but incorrect for Appraisal; the student did not *rate* the characters. This confusion occurs often and underscores the importance of using cue words that target a specific kind of response. It also shows the value of teaching students the Questions for Life model, which allows teachers to literally point to the cue words that apply to desired thinking processes so students can learn to think consciously and purposefully.

Appraisal questions or statements ask us to *rank, rate, grade, prioritize,* etc., according to certain criteria—importance, sequence, outcome, etc. A series of Appraisal questions or statements a teacher might ask include the following:

"Let's look at the lists of items that go into our survival kit and *rank* which are the *most* important and which are the *least* important to have in a fire emergency." [Criterion: importance]

"There are five steps in this assignment. *Prioritize* the steps in the order in which you intend to complete them." [Criterion: sequence]

"Can you *rate* the events in the book in terms of how suspenseful they were?" [Criterion: suspense]

"*Appraise* the importance of the gold rushes in California, Colorado, and Alaska in terms of how they contributed to creation of statehood." [Criterion: influence on statehood]

"Let's *grade* the quality of our pies in terms of which ones the first graders eat first!" [Criteria: popularity, taste]

Comparing Appraisal and Evaluation

What is the *same* and what is *different* about Appraisal and Evaluation? Most of our decisions in life are based on these two thinking processes, so it is important to understand the difference between them. A clue to the answer lies in the cue words. In Appraisal we are *weighing, rating, ranking, grading,* and *prioritizing.* When we Evaluate, we come from our *belief, point of view, judgment, opinion,* or personal *decision.* A substantial analysis must be completed prior to Appraisal to ensure its accuracy, and a well-thought-out *appraisal* leads to better *summaries* and *evaluations.*

Appraisal, then, can be considered more quantitative, while Evaluation is more qualitative; Appraisal is objective, while Evaluation is subjective. Appraisal uses applications related to how we *weigh* or *rank* things; Evaluation is concerned with personal criteria related to how we *judge* and feel about things. Ideally, an *evaluation* is based on *appraising* each aspect of a subject, summarizing its most important points, and then making a *judgment*—the *evaluation.*

A student might buy an iPhone, for example, thinking he had made an *appraisal* of all other phones and methods of obtaining information. In reality, though, he may have already placed a special value on the iPhone—maybe he even lusted after it! He may have *weighed, rated,* and *ranked* all its features only after he bought it, using a type of thinking more like justification and rationalization than true Appraisal.

The student is not alone; many of us base *decisions* on our *beliefs* and *judgments* rather than on a true *appraisal.* An *appraisal* (*ranking* and *weighing* considerations from *best to worst, most to least*) may have influenced the *decision* we already made, but Appraisal itself did not make the *decision*—Evaluation did.

There's nothing really wrong with reversing the order of the two, but it's useful to know when our *decisions* are based on our *beliefs* and *opinions* rather than on a true *appraisal.* On the other hand, when teaching students to be prudent buyers, for example, we want to focus them on using Appraisal before Evaluation because it's a more objective thinking process; at least they should understand the difference between the two. Many salespeople are trained to notice our "buying signs"—behaviors that indicate we are moving toward deciding to make a purchase. To shore up that potential decision, they may *appraise* the various attributes of their product, *weighing* its value against that of competitors' products. Our students' ability to conduct their own independent *appraisal* gives them the unbiased rationale they may need to make a sensible purchase (or to make other kinds of *decisions* that also involve *opinions* and *beliefs*).

Because we are often asked to *evaluate* objects, ideas, people, stories, problems, or experiences, Evaluation is a valuable life skill. When it is based on multiple *appraisals,* it is a very powerful decision-making tool: "I'll buy that iPhone," "I'll get a peer coach," "I'll take that job," "I'll marry that person."

To elicit Evaluation, a teacher might ask the following questions this way:

> "What *viewpoint* on this new policy should I present to the students?"

> "How would you *judge* this student's behavior for the year?"

> "What is your *opinion* of this new computer?"

> "In your *opinion,* which of the three books demonstrates the best example of character development?"

> "From your *viewpoint,* what should we include in our curriculum?"

> "*Critique* the article we just read, basing your *judgment* on the message the article sends."

As we have seen, Appraisal and Evaluation may overlap: Evaluation can lead to Appraisal, and an *appraisal* can justify an *evaluation*. The line between the two can easily blur, as, for instance, when we are in the process of hiring a new principal, grading students, or conducting an evaluation of a teacher in the classroom.

Suppose, for example, you are part of a committee interviewing candidates applying to become the principal of your school. Basing your decisions on a certain set of criteria, you and your group rank the criteria, assign numerical values to them, and come up with specific scores that will be used to identify the top candidates. In the end, however, you base your decision on more subjective, *evaluative* reasons: you hire a candidate because he or she fulfills a need or fits in well with the culture of the school.

Furthermore, when all is said and done, quite often we base our decisions simply on gut feeling. Intuition comes into play in subtle but powerful ways. As we think through and *appraise* the data on our way to Evaluation, subjective thoughts and feelings creep in, creating a "want" that may override the "must" dictated by that numerical score. It's precisely because we tend to wander into the right brain of subjectivity and intuition that we should be aware of our thinking processes. Appraisal and Evaluation serve as the scaffolding from which intuition—and ultimately decision—can build. There is ample research indicating that our brains process information at a subconscious level. Paying attention to the gut feeling, the *affect,* and how we really feel about something ties right into Evaluation and ultimate Action.

Report cards may seem to be *appraisals,* yet grades (which, incidentally, remain the very last criterion any human resource professional considers in job recruitment) do not reflect whether they are based on work habits and behaviors or on test scores. While in some cases they may reflect a specific point or value system used in Appraisal, in fact, grades often come from *judgments,* a form of Evaluation.

Ditto on *evaluations* of teachers: if a teacher's *evaluations* come out the same every time, then probably the evaluations are *appraisals* of performance based on certain criteria. If they differ from evaluator to evaluator, then they are, in fact, *evaluations—judgments—*based on the evaluators' *opinions, beliefs,* and *decisions* about the teacher's performance.

Evaluation and Change in Education

Creating any real change in education or in any other serious endeavor—making changes in the school's curriculum, say, or revamping a community's social services, wiping out drug abuse, slowing the number of teenage pregnancies, or decreasing global warming—requires that we go beyond data gathering and Appraisal or Analysis to reach people's beliefs and value systems, where they really live. In other words, we need to obtain enough information to make an *evaluation* demonstrating that people are ready to take the plunge and make changes that manifest in action.

Successful implementation always depends on solid critical thinking. In the case of education, teachers must gather empirical information, look at their own perceptions, arrive at generalizations, and have *insights*. This process will allow them to reflect on their own way of thinking and make discoveries on their own.

Evaluation comes steeped in our own visions, beliefs, values, judgments, and opinions, which are complex and often stiff with the glue that has held them together for years, possibly all our lives. Is it possible that our thinking may have become skewed over time or laden with information no longer appropriate or even accurate? Perhaps thinking through the Questions for Life model might reveal the benefits of making changes or of embracing a new belief or point of view.

The point of Questions for Life is not simply to show a model of thinking processes—although that's the first step—but to learn and then instill in ourselves and our students an understanding of the natural way we think so we can operate critically inside or outside the classroom. Once ingrained, Questions for Life is a powerful tool that can be applied naturally to any circumstance, any decision, and any needed or desired change.

Summary

Summarizing is a skill employers almost always look for, as it demonstrates the ability to undertake and articulate complex thinking. One of the reasons employers often find this skill lacking in new hires is that creating a *summary* has taken a backseat in education to gathering data and spending time on Analysis activities borne out of textbooks and curriculum. Often when teachers ask students to *summarize* a story, they respond with an analysis, sequencing events in the plot. But Summary requires a higher level of thinking than that required by sequencing, which can be a simple recitation of facts in a sequence. Since critical thinking, which was once included in high school and college curriculums, has more or less vanished as an academic skill, teachers themselves have come increasingly to accept Analysis for Summary.

Being able to *summarize* means being able to communicate in a concise form. To *summarize,* one needs to organize thoughts and note the key elements or *main points* of an object, idea, event, person, story, problem, situation, or experience. (See Figure 7.4.)

SUMMARY	
Main idea	Condense
Main point	Reduce
Summary	Sum up
Focus	In a nutshell
Summarize	

Figure 7.4

Some Summary questions or statements teachers might ask include the following (cue words are italicized):

"*Sum up* what happened in the story, using only one sentence."

"What was the *main point* of *The Tortoise and the Hare?*"

"*In a nutshell,* what did you learn from the movie on drugs?"

"*Reduce* the two pages to 25 words."

"What was the *focus* of Martin Luther King's life?"

"What is the *main idea* behind studying life cycles?"

"*Summarize* the rules for conjugating these verbs."

"*Condense* this information into a logical synopsis."

When asked in an interview to *summarize* his prior experience in working at a fast-food restaurant, a young would-be employee might recite that he took customers' orders, cleaned the counter, ordered supplies, and provided customer service—Analysis, not Summary. If he answered the Summary question correctly, he might talk about the job's key elements and highlights and *sum up* what he felt were the *main points* of the job, such as a continued *focus* on providing good customer service. Summary provides an opportunity to be clear and concise, a selling point to any potential employer.

How We Summarize

Let's consider an example concerning a field trip to Ground Zero in New York City. (See Figure 7.5 on page 99.) When prompted with a Summary question such as "Can you *sum up* what happened on the field trip to Ground Zero?" the person responding—student or fellow educator—might begin with Perception, recalling what he or she saw, heard, felt, etc., represented by the triangles (instances) in Figure 7.5.

Summary Process

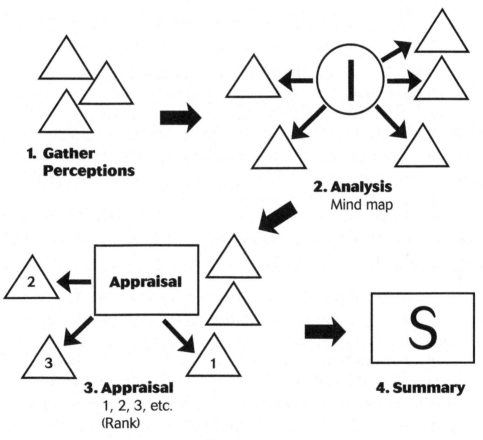

1. Gather Perceptions

2. Analysis
Mind map

Appraisal

3. Appraisal
1, 2, 3, etc.
(Rank)

4. Summary

Figure 7.5

Next the person would probably create a mental mind map, as research shows the brain works in pictures rather than in lists, organizing data through association rather than in a linear process. A mind map is a form of Analysis that captures information in thought balloons: we went to the building site, we looked at the names of those who died, we visited the memorial. It may outline or define what occurred: one woman cried, the construction kept us back from the memorial site, etc. Analysis serves to organize Perception.

A comparison (Same/Different) is very likely to accompany this analysis: the field trip was similar to the one we took to the air museum, but it was different because of the way we felt when we were there. Then the person providing the *summary* might do an appraisal by ranking the most important events that occurred, picking the top three highlights of the trip and weighing the feelings he or she experienced, from best to worst.

Having gone through those various thinking processes, the student or educator might come up with a *summary* like the following:

> We took a field trip to Ground Zero in New York City. We saw where the buildings had been destroyed. We looked at the names of those who died when the planes hit the towers, and we visited the site of the memorial. It was a cold and cloudy day that reflected the emotions of all who went, as most were very quiet and somber. I saw two people crying. It was the most powerful field trip I have ever taken, and one I will never forget.

With that kind of Summary thinking, the kid just might get the job at the hamburger joint!

Figure 7.5 shows a Summary process based on instances leading to Induction, then Analysis, followed by Appraisal and Summary.

We can, however, *summarize* from another place on the Questions for Life model. Starting with an action, we can list the events that occurred (Analysis), weigh them as to how well they were executed (Appraisal), and then *summarize* the entire experience. Because the key to *summarizing* is finding the *main points* from a list, Summary often involves Appraisal and Analysis.

In our discussion about the thinking processes in Row 1 we said we can go from *parts* to a *whole* (Induction) and from a *whole* to *parts* (Analysis). (See Figure 7.6) By the same token, a thought process itself can be a *whole,* and that *whole* can be broken down into *parts.* For example, arriving at an idea (Idea), making a decision (Evaluation), or constructing a plan (Action) can be the *whole,* whose *parts* can then be analyzed: "What occurred as a result of . . .? What steps did we take after . . .?" Once we have broken down the *whole* into *parts,* we can prioritize the *main ideas* (Appraisal) and *condense* them in a *summary* (Summary).

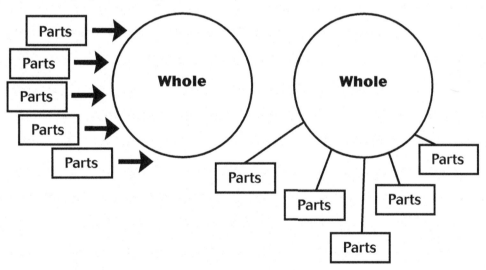

Figure 7.6

The beauty of the Questions for Life model is that all the thinking processes lead naturally into one another. Prediction can lead to a *summary* of what might happen, we can *summarize* insights that we've had, and so on. As Figure 7.7 on page 103 shows, we can start with any thought process (indicated by the tiny Questions for Life shapes within brackets at the top) and subject it to Analysis and Appraisal to achieve a *summary*.

Our Summary Statement

The main point of this discussion is that students, educators, and others who face life's challenges can use Questions for Life to stretch beyond the data, textbook, or situation in front of them to reach out in new ways and create new solutions by learning to think concisely and critically. As our brains think critically, they focus more sharply and become more finely tuned. We are better able to solve complex problems one step at a time and communicate effectively in the global arena.

One culture's complex problem might be to determine how to encourage students to stay in school while helping their parents bring in a valuable harvest; another culture might need to determine a way to retain accountability from employees who work from home in order to decrease pollution caused by commuting; and still another culture might be looking at whether a city should sanction homeless camps or continue to move homeless people into shelters.

Without the ability to think critically, we miss out on many of the natural functions our brains are capable of, taxed to the max as they are with more facts and information than they can ever contain or retain.

Thinking in and of itself, however, is not the ultimate goal of the Questions for Life model. We do not want to get caught in analysis paralysis! The real point of all our great ideas, insights, analyses, appraisals, summaries, and evaluations is to be able to take effective action—to make and do!

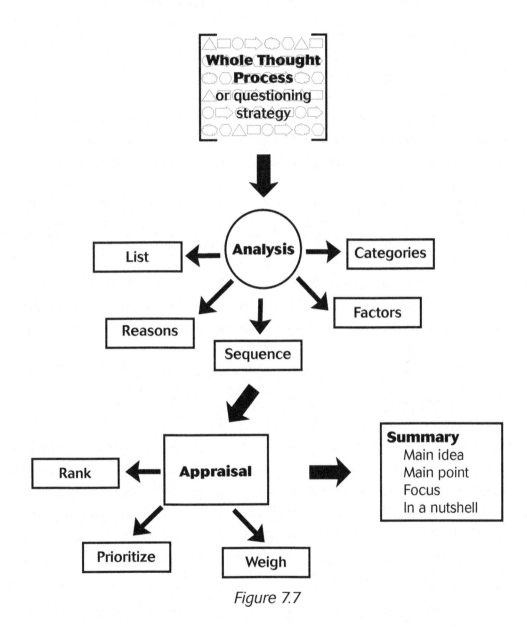

Figure 7.7

Scenario for the Future: Using Rows 1 and 2

Let's go back to the classroom or school of the future in Chapter 6 and look at how combining the questioning strategies in Rows 1 and 2 might move the vision along. In that exercise you visualized the ideal classroom or school of the future (Perception) and then asked your students to do the same. You made an analysis of what might be involved, including a generalization or pattern (Induction) and a comparison (Same/Different) between what exists now and your picture of the future (Perception). Your students, undertaking the same process, arrived at their own generalizations. Together you compared your visions (Same/Different) and arrived at more generalizations or qualities (Induction). And that's where we left off.

Since Questions for Life is a brain-compatible process, you and your students would naturally arrive at an insight—a generalization that connects what you were thinking about to a different generalization, something altogether new (see Figure 7.8 on page 105). Connecting generalizations drives the engine of Insight.

For instance, perhaps you and your students both created a future classroom encompassing qualities or patterns that encouraged students to work independently and collaboratively. Let's say you all envisioned a large room containing separate learning centers or work stations. Seating arrangements varied depending on their location in the room. Many computers equipped with the latest technology provided access to the outside world. The large room also contained a kitchen that served as a place for refreshments and as an area for learning centers for science, math, and nutrition. As teacher and students reflect and allow the inspiration of Insight to occur, the following exchange may take place:

> "What *realizations* do we have about this classroom of the future? What *connections* does it have to other places of learning?" asks the teacher.

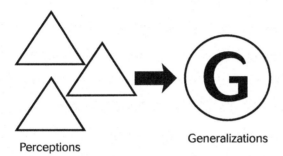

Perceptions   Generalizations

Induction

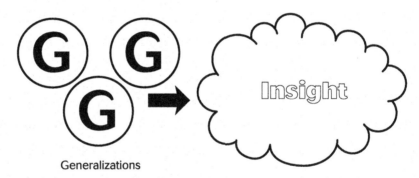

Generalizations

Figure 7.8

"It's sort of like a spaceship," says one elementary school student. "Everything we need is right here, and it has lots of cool technology."

"It reminds me of a studio," chimes in a high school student. "It's like an art studio, but with different types of learning occurring in different areas."

"To me it resembles a laboratory," the teacher suggests. "I think of it as a working laboratory where we can experiment and work together or independently with resources at our fingertips."

(See page 107 Figure 7.9)

These are all insights, connecting what earlier Perception, Induction, Analysis, Same/Different, Appraisal, and Summary devised. You might conduct a further analysis of your ideal classroom or school of the future with your students by mind mapping or listing all its aspects or by comparing (Same/Different) students' pictures of how independent study might be the same or different from your own (Perception). You could then prioritize these aspects (Appraisal) as to feasibility and desirability (or vice versa!). Having weighed, ranked, compared, and prioritized what would be the most important things to have in this classroom (Appraisal), you could then summarize the main ideas you agree on and decide if you want to invest in making some of these changes available in your school (Evaluation).

Critical Thinking and Life

Before continuing on with the Questions for Life model and its implications for teaching, it might be wise to step back and recall that

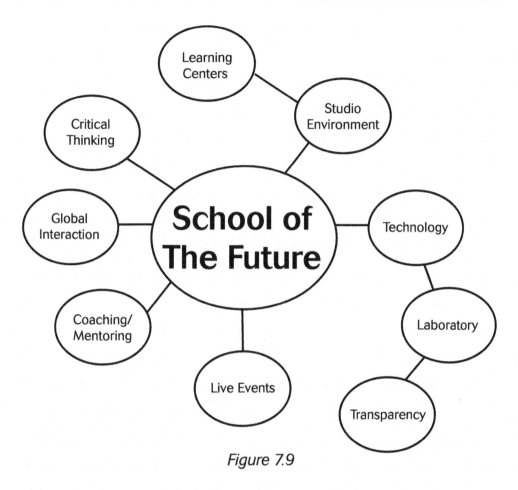

Figure 7.9

the overall purpose of using the model is to be able to take effective action that is based on a solid foundation of critical thinking.

As stressed in earlier chapters, there remains a crucial need for students and educators to be able to apply skills, to think through and around problems, and to embrace current and future twenty-first-century challenges. Doing so will certainly involve making complex choices, communicating clearly, and understanding connections between disparate parts. The ability to analyze and solve problems—quite possibly without any prior information at hand other than what the student can discern—can be greatly aided by gathering data using the questioning strategies outlined in Questions for Life.

While Questions for Life provides a wonderful tool to use in a classroom to help students understand what kind of thinking they are using at any given time, its real importance lies in its name: Questions for *Life*. Life has no curriculum, no lesson plan. When situations occur, we must act or react by using our brains.

Because the Questions for Life model represents a brain-compatible process, once its thinking or questioning strategies are specifically named, regularly practiced, and sufficiently used, they will cause the brain to grow and strengthen. Flowing naturally among the various processes, critical thinking will move out from the purely academic realm and into the greater world where twenty-first-century life and its growing challenges await our response.

Summary

Once again, using Questions for Life allows for movement to and from basic and complex thinking processes, and we can see that each movement builds on the one that precedes it: perceptions are more specific, generalizations are more clear, lists lengthen, analyses become increasingly exacting, summaries are more concise, opinions are based more reliably on data, and insights are therefore ever more stunning. Once we come to the place of believing or deciding that a course of action is needed—once everyone's evaluation is congruent—then we have no choice but to act. And acting is what Questions for Life Row 3 is all about.

Chapter 8
Lights, Camera, Action!
QFL Row 3

Row 3: Think, Then Act

If you think students might have a hard time producing a sound summary, imagine a beginning teacher who is told, "Summarize your fourth-grade social studies curriculum for us." This new teacher has had no time to acquire instances or experiences (to perceive what is going on), to arrive at generalizations, or to analyze the curriculum or evaluate it in any way. Summarizing it would be difficult at best, and such a summary, perhaps based only on what the teacher has read or been told, would probably not reflect what the curriculum actually contained.

Taking the poor beginning teacher one step further, imagine that someone asked her to write lesson plans for the same fourth-grade social studies classes. This would throw her directly into Row 3 of Questions for Life—the row that creates *action*—without addressing Rows 1 and 2 first. Moving directly into *action* without passing "go" is not at all uncommon. It happens in businesses, schools, organizations, and in our own lives. Instead of "Ready, Aim, Fire," the immediate call to *action* suggests, "Fire, Aim, Ready." In Chapter 5 we referred to the "Circle of Assumptions" developed by Eric F. Douglas in *Straight Talk: Turning Communication Upside Down for Strategic Results at Work*. According to Douglas:

> People communicate all the time at the level of actions. Actions seem like the most natural and fluid things in the world. We are so swept up by actions that we neglect their often tenuous connection to facts. People who take action are seen as competent leaders. We forget that actions are based on conclusions, which are based on evaluations, which are based on interpretations, which are based on data.[1]

It follows, therefore, that if we work through the Questions for Life critical thinking skills before we dive into writing lesson plans (or buying a house or changing school districts or creating a science project), we have a much better chance to take *action* that will be effective and successful. Because thinking occurs at lightning speed, stopping to review before moving to Action is a habit worth developing.

That said, it is perfectly natural to jump to Row 3 (see Row 3 in Figure 8.1 on page 111) with an *idea,* a *prediction,* or an *action* and then step back and review it after the fact. The important thing is to make sure that we *do* step back and review by applying additional thought processes. Questions for Life moves and flows that way. Once we become aware that we have landed on an *idea* that might lead to *action,* we need to pause to review its ramifications (employing Analysis, Appraisal, Evaluation, Prediction, etc.). Using the Questions for Life model, we also need to take time to monitor our thought processes as they occur. When working with others in particular, it is very important to make sure that the Evaluation process in

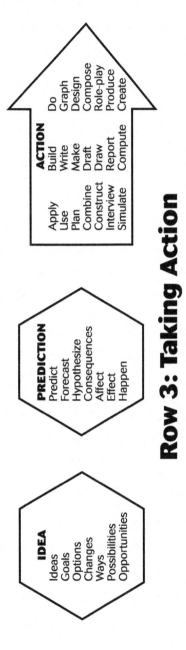

Row 3: Taking Action

Figure 8.1

Row 2 has resulted in agreement, so that everyone *believes* in or has *decided* on how to proceed before moving to Action in Row 3.

As we have said, the ultimate purpose of thinking processes, regardless of sequence, is to enable us to take effective *action*. Without *action,* thinking is only a mental exercise. And without thinking about our thinking before we take *action,* we lose out on the tremendous enlightenment such thinking bestows, running the risk that our *action* will end in futility. So let's jump down now to the exciting Questions for Life Row 3.

Idea

Just as insights sometimes seem to come out of the clouds, *ideas,* too, often arrive mysteriously. They may derive from prior thoughts and experiences, or perhaps from divine inspiration or the special spark of creative genius that characterizes us as humans. In the Questions for Life model, Idea is represented in a hexagonal shape to signify synthesis—a blend, a combination, a creation, or a fusion of thoughts crystallized into an *idea.* (See Figure 8.2) Prediction is likewise housed in a hexagonal shape because *ideas* and predictions often occur simultaneously or in swift succession, one after the other.

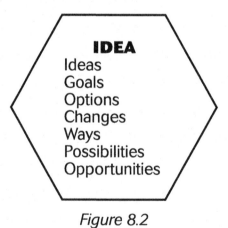

IDEA
Ideas
Goals
Options
Changes
Ways
Possibilities
Opportunities

Figure 8.2

While Analysis questions arise from known facts, Idea questions speculate. The purpose of asking them is to bring about *ideas, goals, ways, options, changes,* or *possibilities* geared to change or improve a situation, lifestyle, or culture. Idea questions ask us—and our students—to take the information we have gathered and ponder how that information can be used in new and creative *ways*.

Using the Questions for Life cue words, Idea questions stimulate students at all levels, from primary to postsecondary. The following examples illustrate ways to pose Idea questions:

"What are some *ways* we could add or take away the blocks?"

"Think of *ideas* for a new game."

"What *goals* should we set for finishing our volcano research?"

"What *options* do we have for places to go on a field trip?"

"If you had an opportunity to advise the President on education policy, what *changes* would you suggest?"

"Think of other *ways* to explain achievement motivation among men and women."

"What low-cost *options* are available to improve the environment?"

Using a relatively recent approach to training and organizational development known as Appreciative Inquiry, those involved seek *ideas* to meet challenges by asking about past experiences that turned out well (Induction). Idea questions are framed that incorporate an expression of how past successes might lead to new *options, possibilities,* or *opportunities* for success in meeting current challenges. This future-seeking approach, based on positive experience, provides a refreshing diversion from Analysis. It stimulates *ideas* and predictions that focus on *possibilities* rather than on breaking down past problems to find and fix the broken parts. Analysis is a viable problem-solving process, too, of course, but its focus is limited. In fact, Idea and Prediction need not apply to problem solving at all, since often when *possibilities* or *opportunities* are sought, the point is to stimulate thinking about something that has yet to be created.

In our classrooms or schools of the future, we looked for *possibilities* and *opportunities* that reflected the successes of the past without actually stating that there was an existing problem with the status quo. An improved school environment can come about simply because someone has a new *idea,* just as better highways, airplanes, and cars are built because engineers see ways to improve upon what exists. Companies change and improve products frequently just to attract new buyers and to have something different to offer each season. The ever-changing nature of technology stems from a constant flow of *ideas* about how to make things better, not from problems inherent in existing versions.

Idea questions in our lives might include:

"What *options* do I have for *ways* to present this idea to the board?"

"What *possibilities* exist to get a grant for improving this laboratory environment?"

"What *changes* can I make to be more motivated in my career?"

Prediction

As soon as we think of a new option or discover an opportunity to do something different, our minds automatically wonder what would *happen* if it occurred—we click into Prediction. And as soon as we *predict* the probable *consequences* of our ideas, the ways in which they might be good or bad usually become apparent: "What might *happen* if we decide upon a particular option? What would be the *consequences* of implementing it in a particular way? And if the *consequences* are not favorable, what other possibilities exist? (Idea)" (See Figure 8.3)

Without using the thinking skill Prediction, we may allow a new idea to die an untimely death, especially if the action we take on the idea fails at first launch. When that happens, we are tempted to revert to the comfort zones of Rows 1 and 2: "Well, it was a good idea, but it didn't work. So let's not do anything right now." Predicting possible *consequences* can help us avoid such failure and encourage us to consider options. Thus does change occur (Row 3's specialty). Idea questions spark creativity, inventiveness, imagination, ingenuity, and originality in ourselves, our colleagues, and certainly in our students. From ideas *predictions* are formed; from *predictions* new ideas and possibilities arise.

Figure 8.3

In his book *Good to Great,* Jim Collins recites a story he calls "The Stockdale Paradox."[2] It's the story of Admiral Jim Stockdale, a high-ranking officer captured and held for eight years in the horribly brutal "Hanoi Hilton" prison camp in Vietnam. Admiral Stockdale was tortured repeatedly. Left without any prisoners' rights or release date, he struggled and sacrificed throughout the years to help fellow captives in his command to survive unbroken.

Stockdale did survive and lived to tell about it in his book *In Love and War,* written in collaboration with his wife, with whom he corresponded in code, exchanging secret intelligence throughout those eight painful years.[3] Collins and one of his students, who was writing a paper about Stockdale for a philosophy class, arranged an interview with Stockdale. Asked how he had survived while others perished, Stockdale said those who did not make it out were the optimists. Confused, Collins and his student probed further, and Admiral Stockdale pointed out that the optimists kept saying, "We'll be out by Christmas" and then "We're going to be released at Easter" or "Here's to Thanksgiving" or New Year's or whatever—and each time an event came and went without release, the resolve of the optimists diminished, and many died of broken hearts.

This tragic yet hopeful story shows the power of Prediction when we look at both the positive and the negative *consequences* of an idea or an action. The prisoners had a need to be optimistic about getting released—it was something they considered necessary to hold onto. Yet they also could have considered the facts, the situation, and the negative possibilities—that they may, in fact, stay another painful year. In doing so, they may have achieved the odd balance—the paradox—that could have ensured their survival.

The "Stockdale Paradox" affirms: "Retain faith that you will prevail in the end, regardless of the difficulties, *AND AT THE SAME TIME* confront the most brutal facts of your current reality, whatever they may be."

In life we often make only optimistic *predictions,* yet the results of the actions we take based on those *predictions* can be positive or negative. (See Figure 8.4) Positive *predictions* live in the realm of visualization, where we picture outcomes as glowingly success-ful. *Predicting* allows us to plan, for better or for worse.

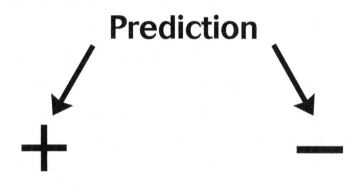

Figure 8.4

Coming up with an idea for change and then *predicting* the best possible outcome as well as all that could go wrong allows us to *predict* the future more accurately. Picturing or acknowledging the worst-case scenario allows us to focus our energies on making the positive happen, while letting negative possibilities hover in the background unaddressed keeps them there in limbo, distract-ing us from positive forward movement. Prediction enables us to face potential downfalls and get them out of the way. As Alan Loy McGinnis notes in his book *The Power of Optimism,* optimists are never surprised by trouble.[4]

Prediction questions invite a *forecast* or a *hypothesis.* They play the game "What if?" citing the possible implications of proposed actions: "What might *happen? How will A affect B?* If we do this, what do you suppose the *consequences* will be?"

Keep in mind that Questions for Life is a brain-compatible process, which means that our brains will go through many of the thinking processes whether we are aware of them or not. However, when we focus on the cue words to elicit the processes consciously, and when we let our students *know* that we're doing so, we're able to augment the dynamic advantages the thinking processes afford.

Here are questions for primary students that guide Prediction. Whether these young ones understand the concept of Prediction or not, their brains will respond appropriately to questions that include the cue words.

> "If Baby Bear spills the porridge, what might *happen?*"

> "What would *happen* if we took something that did not belong to us?"

While using the word *prediction* or *consequences* in primary school might be premature, it is appropriate for children at the elementary and middle school levels. The following statements are ways to brief a lesson for these students:

> "*Predict* how you would feel about taking a job in a foreign country."

> "Basing your answer on the title, *predict* what might *happen* in the story."

> "*Forecast* how the weather would change if all the continents were linked."

> "*Hypothesize* how the South would be different if the Civil War had not occurred."

Students in high school and postsecondary schools would ideally have been taught the Questions for Life model and could therefore move easily to the appropriate thought process once a cue word was used. Questions they could respond to with Prediction might include:

> "Here are the equation Y=2X and its graph in the coordinate plane. What would *happen* to the graph if you replaced the 2 with a 3?"

> "What *effect* will changing these notes have on the overall composition?"

> "*Predict* how taking a technical arts class would change your life."

In our own lives we may naturally ask ourselves:

> "What might *happen* if I decide to get professional coaching?"

> "What *effect* will adding more visuals to this presentation have on my class?"

> "How would it *affect* my students if I were to greet each one of them at the door each day?"

> "What would be the *consequences* of sharing my frustrations with my colleague?"

Idea and Prediction

Because the Idea process allows us to synthesize information, crystallize it, and bring forth new *goals, options, opportunities,* or *possibilities,* the *idea* itself typically goes through a natural, brain-compatible process. You may recall that we looked at Perception from the point of view of a crime scene investigator who began an investigation by limiting examination of the evidence to only what could be seen, heard, smelled, touched, or otherwise detected with the senses. Advancing to the Idea process in Row 3, we can now bring a higher level of thinking to the investigation. At this stage the investigator can perform all the following critical thinking processes: look carefully at the evidence (Perception) and note a pattern in how the crime was committed (Induction), recall past experiences with similar patterns (Same/Different), analyze the entire situation (Analysis), prioritize clues in order of importance (Appraisal), summarize the evidence (Summary), make a judgment about it (Evaluation), begin to look for ways to solve the case or at least come up with possibilities for further investigation (Idea), and predict the likelihood of success (Prediction). Having thoroughly thought through the entire case in this way, the investigator can then confidently take action (Action).

A similar thinking pattern is required if we are to respond successfully to the crucial questions that confront our planet today. Faced with challenging issues like climate change and genetically engineered foods, scientists and other leaders would do well to undertake a process of critical thinking similar to that of our investigator before they decide to jump on an idea and take action. Using critical thinking to probe ideas whose positive and/or negative consequences can be predicted with reasonable accuracy is crucial for those who hope to act successfully on behalf of our challenged world.

Action

Does this mean that we can't take *action* until we go step-by-step through all the Questions for Life? Of course not! Questions for Life is about *life,* and taking *action* can be exhilarating, creative, and fun. Those familiar with learning styles will appreciate that kinesthetic learners often move first to Action: "Let's just do it and think about it later!" (See the Action cue words in Figure 8.5.) Those who have used Performance Learning Systems' learning and working styles inventory *The Kaleidoscope Profile®* will understand why people whose perceptual and organizational styles are concrete and global might also be more action-oriented, letting their abstract and sequential colleagues go through the thinking process step-by-step.[5] Sensing Perceivers from the Myers-Briggs Temperament Types are also likely to move first to Action.[6] There is room for everyone in Questions for Life!

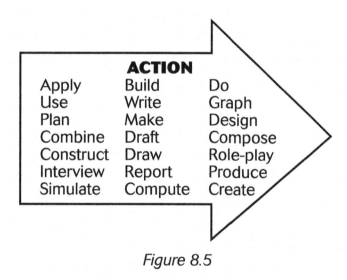

Figure 8.5

Going With the Flow

So here we are at Action, the end of the Questions for Life model. But not so fast! Once *action* is taken—once ideas are *applied,* plans *drawn,* reports *written,* or classrooms *designed,* we must, alas, go immediately back to Row 1 and start over again, as depicted in Figure 8.6 on page 122. *Action* begets more thought that leads to more *action,* but before we can *create* and *do* and *produce* more, we need to—you guessed it—go to Rows 1 and 2 to gather data, work with it, and build a solid foundation.

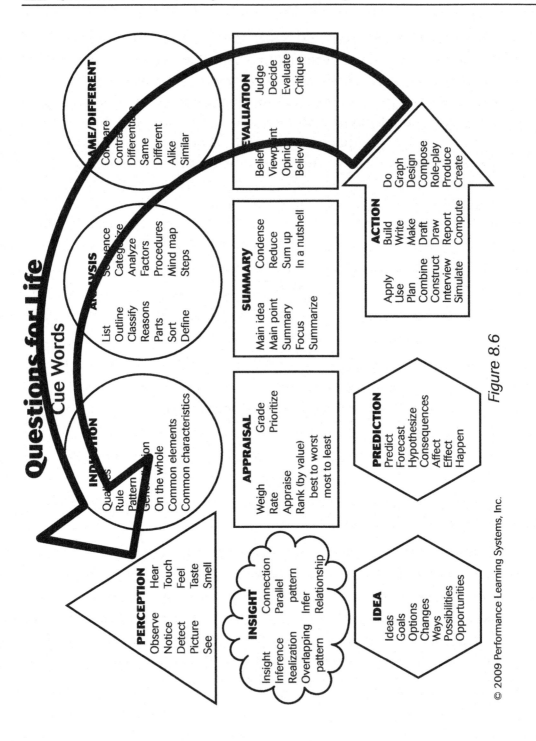

Questions for Life
Cue Words

PERCEPTION

Observe   Hear
Notice   Touch
Detect   Feel
Picture   Taste
See   Smell

INDUCTION

Qualities
Rule
Pattern
Generalization
On the whole
Common elements
Common characteristics

ANALYSIS

List   Sequence
Outline   Categorize
Classify   Analyze
Reasons   Factors
Parts   Procedures
Sort   Mind map
Define   Steps

SAME/DIFFERENT

Compare
Contrast
Differentiate
Same
Different
Alike
Similar

EVALUATION

Belief   Judge
Viewpoint   Decide
Opinion   Evaluate
Believe   Critique

SUMMARY

Main idea   Condense
Main point   Reduce
Summary   Sum up
Focus   In a nutshell
Summarize

ACTION

Apply   Do
Use   Build   Graph
Plan   Write   Design
Combine   Make   Compose
Construct Draft   Role-play
Interview Draw   Produce
Simulate   Report   Create
           Compute

APPRAISAL

Weigh
Rate   Grade
Appraise   Prioritize
Rank (by value)
best to worst
most to least

PREDICTION

Predict
Forecast
Hypothesize
Consequences
Affect
Effect
Happen

INSIGHT

Insight   Connection
Inference   Parallel
Realization   pattern
Overlapping   Infer
pattern   Relationship

IDEA

Ideas
Goals
Options
Changes
Ways
Possibilities
Opportunities

Figure 8.6

© 2009 Performance Learning Systems, Inc.

Continuing with our investigation example, once the suspect has been apprehended (once *action* has been taken), the investigator immediately goes back to Perception and makes careful observations, noting what the suspect looks like and says. The investigator thinks of similar suspects, notices patterns, makes comparisons, lists reasons for questioning witnesses, and sequences how those reasons led to the *action* that was taken. In short, using Perception, Induction, Analysis, and Same/Different, the investigator gathers additional data in order to implement further Action.

At that point the investigator may see a similarity from a prev-ious case and have an insight about how the crime was com-mitted. Jumping to Evaluation, the investigator may decide to follow up on this insight by going out and *interviewing* key witnesses again. Then the investigator may decide to back off, predicting what might happen if one of the witnesses were in cahoots with the suspect. This brings up another idea, and then . . .

You can see the pattern.

But can your students see one? And how can you keep all these moving, flowing thought processes clear in their minds?

An example of one way Questions for Life can move and flow is depicted in Figure 8.7 on page 124. Notice how Analysis sits at the center of this graphic. Analysis is often the starting point when we tackle an issue, a problem, a decision, or a plan: we mentally list the elements involved and pick the one that "needs doing." We gather the information. From there, the mind goes to other thought processes, and it does so by creating questioning strategies.

For example, let's say that within your school you have an option to start a new job that has a lot more variety and challenge than your current job, but your pay would fluctuate according to how often you are required to perform the new task. The job you have now enjoys a steady income.

Questions for Life
Possible Flow of Questioning or Thought Processes

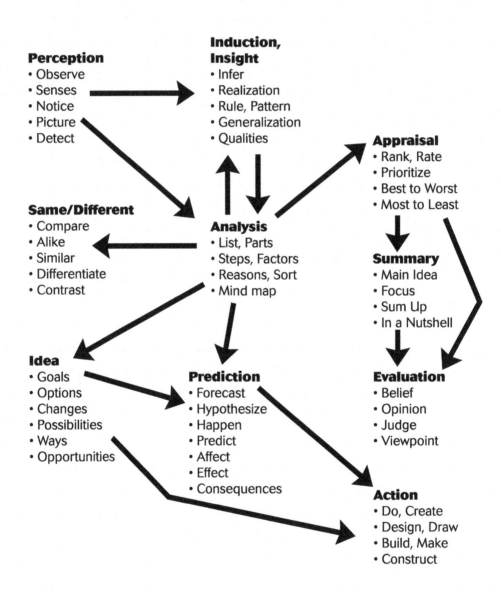

Figure 8.7

Developed by Angelo Rivera

Using the Questions for Life model, you might start with Analysis:

"For what *reasons* would I take the new job?"

"*List* the pros and cons of the two positions."

Then you might move to Appraisal:

"*Prioritize* the pros and the cons, determining the top three in each category."

Same/Different:

"How would I *compare* this new job to my current job?"

To develop this comparison, you could carry out a strategy known as Voice Dialogue[7]: sit in a chair, close your eyes, and visualize yourself in the new job. Observe what you are doing, notice feelings and hear sounds (Perception). Then share your feelings aloud with someone in the room, with someone you imagine, or with yourself:

"I see myself smiling. I feel excitement. I hear applause."

Next, move to a different chair, close your eyes, and visualize yourself remaining in your current job, having turned down the other. See what you are doing, notice feelings, and hear sounds (Perception). Share aloud your feelings:

"I see my classroom of 20 years. I hear others saying I did the right thing to turn down this job. I feel . . ."

Now move to Insight:

> "What *realizations* do I have as a result of doing this activity?"

> "What *insights* do I have about myself?"

You may begin to question yourself, using Evaluation:

> "Do I really *believe* I can do this job?"

Perhaps you move to Idea:

> "Might I have the *option* of performing the service under my existing salary, with perhaps a slight increase?"

And then you make a Prediction:

> "How would retaining my salary and getting paid extra for new tasks *affect* my decision?"

Finally, you are ready for Action! Perhaps you decide to meet with someone to get more ideas, or simply respond to the offer yea or nay.

Bringing this type of thinking into your classroom, you might announce to your students, for example, that you will be giving them an assignment to write about why Anne Frank's story in *The Diary of Anne Frank*[8] resonates with so many people. Or perhaps your assignment will be for your students to create a nutritional meal for people at the local senior citizens' center, or to do a project involving math, science, history, or any other subject requiring critical thinking. You then share with your students that there is a preliminary task they must begin with *before* they tackle the assignment: they must ask themselves and others a series of critical thinking questions, using the Questions for Life model as a guide.

Another example of how you can help students think critically might occur when a student is deciding whether to join a social group. You can suggest that the student step back and list the questions that need to be asked before coming to a final decision: "What do I notice about this group? How does it make me feel? How is it different from other groups? How is it similar? What insights do I have? What connections can I make? How do I weigh the importance of being in this group compared to participating in other activities? How can I summarize what the group means to me? What do I believe about it? What are my other options? What predictions, good and bad, can I make about what might happen if I join? And what action can I take (or, in this case, not take) to achieve a successful outcome?"

Different problems and opportunities require different questions, of course, but thinking critically beforehand, no matter what the topic—tackling an assignment, making a decision, planning an event, creating an idea—affords tremendous advantage when it comes time to take final action.

Working with our students in this way also provides opportunities for collaboration that help put to rest the old top-down teaching style that no longer works in our modern world. Student and teacher can work together posing questions, perhaps one to the other, to ensure that thinking is on target and that they understand each other's intentions.

Giving students more ownership and empowering them to think for themselves, helped by our guidance, are the new requirements of contemporary education. Embracing Questions for Life and its cue words starts and supports the process.

Teachers have the most to gain by applying Questions for Life thinking strategies to their own lives, both in and out of the classroom. Integrating the strategies into their own thinking and then enabling students to master these critical thinking tools could very well be the single most powerful gift they can give their students and the most important teaching achievement of their year.

Briefing and Debriefing

The questioning strategies in Questions for Life that occur *before* Action are for purposes of **briefing** the students—giving them a heads-up about what information they might want to gather: "Notice X (Perception). Compare Y with Z (Same/Different). Look for over-lapping patterns (Insight)."

Debriefing, too, occurs as the lesson, project, live event, or action unfolds. During the event we might use Row 1 questions, such as "What do you see? How is this similar to or different from . . . ? What were the steps involved?" After the action is completed, debriefing questions serve to solidify knowledge, assess the project, or glean subject matter from the live event: "What was your opinion of . . . ? (Evaluation) What do you think might happen if . . . ? (Prediction) What was the best and what was the worst thing that happened? (Appraisal)"

We will work more with briefing and debriefing in Chapter 9, where we will explore methods of teaching Questions for Life.

Chapter 9
Questions for Life in the Classroom
Questions for Life in Primary School

Seventeen small children are busy chatting and wiggling and squirming in their desks in Ms. Clark's first-grade classroom. She announces that they are going to do a learning activity to continue their study of trains, and she points to a large poster on the wall showing a train from engine to caboose, including all the cars between.

As the students are talking excitedly, Ms. Clark asks each of them to pretend to be one of the *parts* of the train—a car, the engine, or the caboose. She requests that they stand up, come quietly to the front of the room, and line up in the same *sequence* as a train. To help them, she refers to the poster.

"I want to pretend we are a choo-choo train, just like the poster," she says. "Each of you represents one *part* of the train. So please line up one right after the other in a *sequence*."

She models this by placing two students together, one behind the other, starting with the student who is the engine. One by one the remaining students form a line at the front of the room, facing the wall with the poster.

"What's at the front of a train?" she asks.

"The engine!" the students cry.

"Which end of our line is the engine?" she asks, and the child on the right says, "Me!"

"What's at the back of the train?"

"The caboose!" answer the students.

"If John is the engine at the beginning of our train, who's the caboose?"

The child at the other end says, "I'm the caboose!"

"The rest of the train has *parts* that carry different things. People who make trains call these parts 'cars.' Do they look like cars?"

"No!" the students shout.

"What is the *same* and what is *different* about cars and these *parts* that make up the train?"

"The train *parts* look like boxes. Cars aren't boxes," points out one student.

"Cars have wheels and the train *parts* have wheels, so that's the same," says another.

"My daddy's car is in the garage, and these are all in a line. So these cars are *different* from my daddy's car."

"Very good!" smiles the teacher. "The *parts* of a train, called cars, are together in a *sequence,* just as we are standing here in a *sequence*.

"One part of the train holds the baggage. This is called the 'baggage car.' "Baggage" means the items that passengers brought with them on the train, such as their suitcases. Other *parts* hold mail—letters and packages people send one another. Passengers sit in most *parts* of the train, and those *parts* are called 'passenger cars.' Another *part* is a dining room where passengers eat their lunch while they travel. Who wants to be the *parts* of our train that hold the baggage? We need two volunteers."

Two children raise their hands.

"Great, these two *parts* are baggage cars. They're behind the engine, one right after the other, in a *sequence*. You two get in line behind the engine so you are lined up in a *sequence*.

"And who wants to be the passenger cars, the *parts*—or cars— that hold the people?"

Several children raise their hands.

"On our train the passenger cars follow the baggage cars, so get into the correct *sequence* by following the baggage cars.

"Great! Now all we need is a mail car, the only *part* missing from our *sequence*. Janice, you haven't raised your hand. Do you want to be the *part* of the train that carries the mail?"

"I want to be the caboose!" she pouts.

"If you pretend you're the mail *part* of the train this time, you can be the caboose next time we play, okay? The mail car can be right before the caboose. So move into that *sequence*."

Ms. Clark is teaching Analysis by teaching the concept of *sequencing* and *sorting parts,* pointing out what is the *same* and what is *different.* Using a Questions for Life Cue Words poster, she points to it and tells her students that *sequencing* is Analysis.

On another day Ms. Clark brings in an assortment of candies— hard candies, jelly beans, and chocolates—and asks her students to put them into *categories.* As she points to the poster, she tells them that *sorting* and putting candy into *categories* is also Analysis.

The next day she reads the students a story and then asks them to recount to her what happened at the story's beginning. Then she asks what happened next, in the middle of the story. Finally she asks what happened at the end. She points out that the story, like the train, has *parts* in a *sequence.* Then she asks the students if they can tell her what the *main point,* or the *main idea,* of the story is. Since the children now have a more thorough understanding of *sequence,* they are able to progress to the higher-level critical thinking embedded in a Summary question.

Even in first grade (and Kindergarten before that) students can grasp the kinds of critical thinking the teacher is asking them to do simply because these thinking processes are a natural part of our DNA. Thinking in sequence is something we do, and we can begin at a young age to develop critical thinking skills by experiencing how one thought process leads to another.

Primary students can answer a question or respond to a statement by hearing a cue word and seeing it graphically depicted in a poster. For example, Analysis can be shown as a mama bunny with several bunnies lined up beneath her, or Perception can be shown as an eyeball focused on a flower. The following kinds of questions help primary students learn to think critically:

> "What do you *see* in the bowl?" (Perception)

> "What color do you *notice?*" (Perception)

> "You have seen them on the rocks. You've heard their bark. What do these *characteristics* tell you they are?" (Induction)

> "Tell me about the *parts* of this fish." (Analysis)

As students get older, they can continue to use the same Questions for Life cue words, but they will be able to make more connections between the cue words and the thinking required, as follows:

> "If you're asking for *options,* Ms. Younkins, you're asking me to use Idea."

> "If you're asking for *consequences,* you want my *predictions,* right?"

The world needs critical thinkers more than ever before, and the need could well be met by starting with an engine, some cars, and a caboose lined up in sequence!

Questions for Life in High School Literature

In his English classes Mr. Yeates often had trouble with literature discussions. He tended to stick to memory questions relating to facts rather than try to inspire original or critical thinking. Some students in his classes didn't interact, particularly if they hadn't memorized the portion of the book Mr. Yeates was asking about. When he learned about Questions for Life, Mr. Yeates first made a point of applying the system to his own thinking, then started teaching it to his students. He found he began asking them questions in new ways that led to more productive, meaningful discussions, which in turn evoked more in-depth thinking. Students who had once been reticent now found they could share their thoughts because, encouraged to respond with their own interpretations, they no longer had to come up with one "right" answer. They responded with what *they* thought, and more importantly, they were able to explain *how* they arrived at their conclusions. For example, taking his cue from his teacher's question, one student responded: "You said *reason* again. That's another one of those crazy Analysis questions, isn't it, Mr. Yeates?" And he launched into a well-reasoned Analysis.

Mr. Yeates also used Questions for Life to prepare his students before they began work on a writing assignment. By organizing their thinking with a *mind map* as an *analysis* of their *main points,* they were able to produce original work that was both probing and convincing.

From his experience working with Questions for Life in his class-room and in his personal life, Mr. Yeates realized that mere intuitive understanding, while certainly worthwhile, was simply not enough. In an increasingly transparent world, it was more and more necessary to be able to show how a decision, insight, or any other thinking process developed. In addition, he found that Questions for Life produced many cooperative learning opportunities for his students as they shared their ideas and the skillful, conscious thinking that led to them.

Questions for Life in Science

Mr. Rivera stands before his senior high school science class. Behind him on the classroom walls are huge, colorful posters depicting the Questions for Life questioning strategies with their cue words. The posters aid students when Mr. Rivera asks them questions that contain the cue words (and they double as poster-sized cheat sheets for the teacher!). Each poster represents a shape in the Questions for Life model: triangle, circles, rectangles, hexagons, etc. Another poster shows a flow chart of thinking processes centered in Analysis similar to that shown in Figure 8.7 on page 124. This is, after all, a science class.

All of Mr. Rivera's students have studied the thinking processes from the Questions for Life model. Each student has a desk copy of his or her own Questions for Life Cue Words chart similar to the one in the back of this book (and Figure 1.2 on page 12). Because the Questions for Life model consists of a basic template that students of all ages can understand, it makes good sense to share it by giving each student his or her own copy. Consulting the chart, students identify the thinking processes they are using as they solve problems and work their way through experiments.

Mr. Rivera reminds his students to review their Questions for Life cue words as he hands out a lab experiment for them to complete. Included with the lab assignment is another assignment asking students to respond to the statement, "*List* two or three thinking processes you used to arrive at your answer." (An Analysis statement—did we mention this was a science class?) His point in asking them to respond to this statement along with the assignment is for students to figure out how their brains arrive at the answer (i.e., to *analyze* what they do). What *map* do their brains use to get to that decision or solve that problem?

In order to develop the ability to answer questions about their thinking, of course, students had to first learn how to use the Questions for Life strategies consistently. Mr. Rivera devoted one full semester to teaching Rows 1, 2, and 3 of Questions for Life. While his focus was painstaking at first, Mr. Rivera concentrated on being consistent with the cue words, using one in each question so students could understand what type of thinking he was trying to elicit from them. As the cue words became more familiar, the process of conscious critical thinking (metacognition) started to come more naturally to both Mr. Rivera and his students.

As one way to practice the questioning strategies, students were placed in groups of three. Each student took out a sheet of paper and noted one activity he or she enjoyed, such as listening to music, texting friends, playing sports, or connecting to an online social network. The papers were then rotated around the table, and students worked together on each one. Using the Questions for Life Cue Words chart, each student created five relevant questions from five different types of thinking to ask each group member about the activity he or she had noted. As Student A posed questions to Student B, Student C identified the name of the thinking strategy and the cue word used in each question. Once one round was completed, they moved to the next person's activity and then to the next, so that all three students had an opportunity to work with the Questions for Life strategies from different perspectives.

Questions for Life and Careers

Questions for Life provides a powerful way for students to identify the skills and behaviors required in various occupations.

The exercise described below can be undertaken throughout a school year or expanded over several grade levels. If extended, each grade could use increasingly higher levels of thinking to create questions about a variety of occupations. The same could hold true in a single school year, pacing the learning of the different rows of Questions for Life throughout the ongoing months of the year.

For example, students might work on Row 1 exclusively for one month. Together they role-play such different occupations as hairdresser, truck driver, artist, and salesperson. But before their role-plays students use the Questions for Life Cue Words chart to develop questions relevant to the daily tasks of the jobs they're going to portray. Creating these questions ahead of the role-plays serves as a briefing for what they are about to do.

A Perception question for a hairdresser, for example, might be, "What do I *notice* about the way this customer's hair grows?" A mechanic might ask a customer, "What do you *hear* in the engine?" As the students move to Induction, someone playing a business owner might ask, "*On the whole,* what does this financial report tell me about what's happening to my business?" A nurse might ask himself, "What *rules* did I learn in my training about how to keep a surgical procedure sterile?"

Whether moving through one year or up the grades, the level of questioning becomes more complex as students learn more about the skills and thought processes that go into the occupation they have chosen to role-play. A doctor, for instance, might ask a Perception question similar to the one the mechanic asked above: "What do I *hear* in this stethoscope?" And he or she might then move to another level: "What is my *opinion* about this patient's eating habits?" (Evaluation). And then to Row 3: "What will be the *consequences* if he continues with these habits?" (Prediction).

As an alternative, the process of developing questions about occupations using Questions for Life can be taken out into the community as a live event. Students can interview those working in any occupation—sales clerks, dentists, football coaches, attorneys, etc. They may even choose to interview their own parents about the careers they have chosen. The questions designed before the interviews would serve as a briefing; as a debriefing, the students could then redesign the questions after the interviews to reflect the new insights they have gained.

Once an interview is completed, a student might compile a *list* of thinking skills used in the occupation (Analysis) and *summarize* the interviewee's comments to arrive at a *realization* (Insight) about the skills required to do the job. Students' lists could morph to posters and serve as a steady reminder of job opportunities and the types of thinking, skills, and behaviors they entail.

When students get to the point of posing such questions as "What do you think might *happen* if we temporarily stopped funding the space program and applied those funds instead to programs for the homeless?" (Prediction) or "What new opportunities would teachers have if we *decided* to open up a laboratory-like school for multigrades?" (Prediction), they are on their way to understanding the complexities—and the joys—of critical thinking.

Questions for Life Web Site

More ideas for lessons incorporating the Questions for Life model are found in the Appendix of this book, beginning on page 147. In addition, the Web site **www.plsweb.com/QFL** offers an opportunity for continued learning about Questions for Life. Comments, examples of lesson plans, a blog by Stephen G. Barkley, and ideas from teachers, Performance Learning Systems instructors, and others will continue to expand on this site. It is designed to be used by educators and students alike, so feel free to visit often!

Begin With Yourself

First Step: Understand Questions for Life

Learning the thinking processes and the cue words that represent them comes first in the process of teaching Questions for Life. It may feel awkward at first to dissect your thinking processes, give them names, and remember their shapes. But because the strategies represent our natural thinking patterns, they are easy to grasp. And the reward is great—they are incredibly helpful when working to develop a plan, create a solution, or make a decision. And while not all-inclusive, they reflect the ways of thinking we use most often.

Second Step: Practice

The second step is to practice the thinking processes in as many situations as you can—whether you are grocery shopping, designing a lesson plan, opening a 401(k), or adopting a kitten. And, again, this can be accomplished by using the concepts of briefing and debriefing. Before you decide, act, or agree, brief yourself by creating the questions you need to ask yourself. Keep them in your head or write them down. You might start by asking, "What Questions for Life thinking processes would serve me in this situation?" Or you could create a list of needs (Analysis) and then develop questions from those needs to lead you to ultimate Action.

Briefing and Debriefing Your Own Process

Figure 9.1 on page 139 shows a problem-solving process called The Solution Seeking Cycle that comes from a Performance Learning Systems graduate course titled *Behavioral, Academic, and Social Interventions for the Classroom.*[1] The course uses

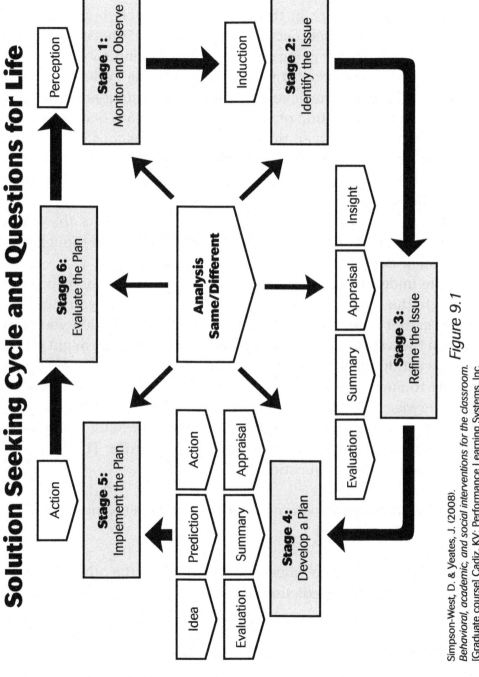

Solution Seeking Cycle and Questions for Life

Figure 9.1

Simpson-West, D. & Yeates, J. (2008).
Behavioral, academic, and social interventions for the classroom.
[Graduate coursel Cadiz, KY: Performance Learning Systems, Inc.

Questions for Life to plan interventions with students. Analysis and Same/Different are in the center of the cycle because these two thinking processes occur at each stage of the intervention process, as the arrows going out from the center indicate. The other thinking processes occur at various stages of the cycle.

Figure 9.1 depicts the development of a plan intended to address an issue. In this depiction observation (Perception) occurred early in the process and moved through the Questions for Life model to ultimate Action. Had the situation been different, it's possible that another thinking process would have begun the process, indicated by a different flow of thinking in the Solution Seeking Cycle. The point is to stop and *brief* yourself at the beginning of the cycle, using questioning strategies that will lead to a well-thought-out solution or decision.

While undertaking an action, you can also *debrief* as you move through the cycle, asking yourself the questions you need to either gather more information or weigh the information you have against the way the action is unfolding (Appraisal). You might evaluate the action in midcourse and decide to start over, or you might decide to move ahead. Once you have decided, planned, created, or otherwise taken action, you can debrief what you have done by asking Questions for Life to determine how successful the process was or what you might do differently in the future. The following are examples of such questions:

> "What were the *parts* of the lesson that I felt went well?" (Analysis)

> "What might have *happened* if I had taken the other apartment?" (Prediction)

> "If I could *condense* that whole process, how would I describe what happened?" (Summary)

Briefing and debriefing can be compared to standing beside a sparkling blue lake on a summer's day, deciding whether or not to dive in. Briefing yourself might include testing the temperature of the water, looking to see who else is in or near the lake, and throwing a rock to see how deep the water is. All of these preliminary investigations are analogous to setting yourself up, or briefing, using Questions for Life. Once in the water, you might debrief by asking yourself how you feel, what the temperature is like, whether you made a mistake or not, what plans you might have to swim across the lake, how deep the water is, etc. Once out and dry, you could reflect on your experience: perhaps you're proud of yourself for taking the swim; maybe you want to bring a friend back with you to experience the water; too bad you didn't bring a sandwich, as now you're hungry. Debriefing with Questions for Life provides a powerful way to reflect.

Third Step: Teach Students to Use Questions for Life

When the process of Questions for Life begins to feel somewhat natural to you, your third step is to teach students how to use it to develop the critical thinking skills they can take out into this dynamically changing world of ours.

Notice the phrase "begins to feel somewhat natural to you" in the above sentence. As we noted earlier, dissecting your thoughts into labeled processes may feel awkward at first. And sometimes we get it wrong. There are nuances to thinking that can make an Evaluation question seem like an Idea question, for example. You may have to take a look at the cue words to ensure that you're using a strategy accurately.

One of the values of the Questions for Life model is that, once a teacher is fairly confident using it, he or she can practice the thinking processes with students by playing with different scenarios and identifying processes together: Was that an Idea question or a prediction? Evaluation or Appraisal? Analysis or Summary? Teaching and learning in concert fine-tunes thinking and makes the process a strategic game that invites excitement and additional learning.

Teaching and Learning

Ah, teaching and learning! What is the *same* and what is *different* about teaching and learning? Both involve facts, knowledge, a desire to know, lessons, assessments, practice—all the aspects of any educational process. This book has been an attempt to teach. We set up compelling reasons to both learn and teach critical thinking skills, and we highlighted schools that were using various forms of teaching to incorporate critical thinking. We focused on teaching strategies—especially questioning, which may be the most complex and frequently used strategy teachers employ. Then we presented the Questions for Life model, first in an overview and then step-by-step. Ostensibly, then, you should now have learned all about Questions for Life and be perfectly capable of applying it in your life and your classroom. Right? In the best of all possible worlds that would be so.

What is different about teaching and learning, however, is depicted in Figure 9.2. Teaching *can* be (but is not always) neat, orderly, sequential, managed, and documented. Theoretically,

Teaching *(Can be)*	**Learning** *(Often is)*
• Neat	• Messy
• Orderly	• Spontaneous
• Sequential	• Nonlinear
• Managed	• Irregular
• Documented	• Complex

Figure 9.2

teachers should be able to summarize what a student needs to learn throughout the school year; divide it into teaching days, weeks, or individual lesson plans; and map out the scope and sequence of the learning process. Done! Nice and neat, right? Or, a teacher can design a lesson plan to teach to a certain standard. Once the lesson plan is delivered and assessed, the teacher, assuming that students learned the standard, might check that lesson off the list. Done again. But in truth, all the teacher knows is that the lesson was taught, not that it was learned. Many schools today focus so heavily on teaching that they have forgotten about learning. Figure 9.2 also shows that, in contrast to teaching, learning is *often* (though not always) messy, spontaneous, nonlinear, irregular, and complex.

So while you may have read and studied every word in this book, you may not have learned the concepts and how to use them as sequentially as the way in which the chapters were laid out. Much learning, in fact, occurs as a delayed reaction. A student may sit attentively in a classroom soaking up knowledge like a sponge, even responding to questions correctly. Yet she may not really "get" what she picked up until later, when, say, she's at the mall with a cousin who happens to say something that sparks a mental connection, causing the information and its meaning suddenly to make perfect sense.

In the same way, skill in using the cue words and the questioning strategies of Questions for Life will develop with use in day-to-day living. You will not always get it right; when you teach it, there may be fuzzy areas. After all, this work is taking place in the brain, which uses thought processes that can occur in microseconds.

In a Nutshell . . .

Teaching and learning occur all the time, at every level, to all of us. One way to teach students or others is to simply go through the

Questions for Life model step-by-step, explaining it and showing how it applies both in and out of school. Teaching it in this way can be a good exercise for a semester or a whole year—Questions for Life can encourage and empower students even if it's taught for only one class period.

One of the strengths of Questions for Life is that it allows students to derive their own answers from their own thinking processes: Insight, Induction, Evaluation, etc. As we have seen, the questioning strategies used in Questions for Life often do not point to one "right" answer. On the contrary, they invite students to create answers based on their own original thinking, an openness that encourages those who feel intimidated by memory-based questions to enter into the discussion.

The value of using Questions for Life increases when teachers model the cue words and critical thinking processes. Sharing how they went through the thinking process and how they self-questioned about or reflected on a decision can demonstrate to students that critical thinking is relevant and applicable to questions and situations they face every day, both inside and outside of school.

Leadership and Questions for Life

Practically by definition, teachers are natural leaders; students, parents, colleagues, and others come to them all day long seeking guidance in a variety of contexts that often include problems for which Questions for Life is a powerful tool. Asking questions aimed at empowering the seeker to find his or her own solution provides a sense of ownership and competence that can help prevent the problem's recurrence. The problem, for example, might come from a colleague who can't get one of her student's parents to help with his homework. Many questions could be posed to this colleague to help her think critically about the issue before she takes action:

"What do you *hear* the parents say when you mention a homework assignment? What tone do you *hear* in their voices when they speak? What body language do you *see?*" (Perception) "What *reasons* have they given for not helping their child?" (Analysis) "How is their reaction to your suggestions *different* from other parents' reactions?" (Same/Different) "Is there a *connection* between the parents' reaction and the student's behavior in school—can you see any *relationship?*" (Insight) "In your *opinion,* what is keeping the parents from helping their son?" (Evaluation)

Questions for Life in Peer Coaching

Because asking appropriate questions is the most important coaching skill of all, those who enjoy a professional coaching relationship will readily see the value of using Questions for Life while coaching or being coached. Questions focused on the coachee's particular concerns, his or her values, the purpose of the lesson, or prediction of success all move and flow around the 11 key questioning strategies in the Questions for Life model.

Let's say a teacher has difficulty motivating his students and has asked for help. A supportive colleague might jump right in with ideas to "fix" the motivation issue. Coaching is not about giving advice, however; rather, it offers guidance, allowing the person being coached to arrive at his or her own ideas. The answer to the coach's question, "What behaviors do you *see* and *hear* when students are motivated?" (Perception), helps both coach and coachee define and analyze the behaviors the teacher seeks to inspire. A teacher might also have a coach observe and track Questions for Life strategies used in a classroom period or lesson and then discuss them later in a debriefing session. The coach can prompt the teacher to think about what he or she does, what he or she wants, and what meaning he or she draws from a topic, a performance, or a student behavior (Induction). The coach can then break each of the teacher's responses down into parts they can both work on (Analysis).

Looking Ahead

As new technology and information availability continue to expand in our world, we rely more heavily on collaboration, personal interaction, and consensus. Using Questions for Life to discover what makes another person tick or to dig a little deeper into a problem can go a long way toward closing gaps and smoothing out conflicts. And as we all know, the world could use a little more understanding among people.

We will not experience world peace, climate change will not go away, nor will conflict in the Middle East be suddenly resolved just because we study Questions for Life. But the ability to think critically will help us to embrace changes with confidence as we work toward those worthy goals. Students who possess this ability are equipped to succeed, whether they are engaged in a personal interaction or in a global marketplace. And who knows what world problems they may someday be able to solve?

Let's forecast a picture of you and your students working together to develop ideas and plans for a classroom or school of the future where challenges will be met in a laboratory-like setting, rich with technology, information, multidisciplines, multigrades, and teams of teachers all working to support one another. In this environment it's possible that your students just might collaborate with you in creating the curriculum that works best for them. They might even take over teaching for you now and then.

Oh, no! Not that! But think it through—maybe this could be a problem you'd really like to have!

Appendix

Questions for Life Lesson Plans

Introduction

One of the benefits of using Questions for Life in the classroom is that it's flexible and easy to apply. Because they're appropriate for any lesson or test at any grade level, the Questions for Life model and cue words offer endless possibilities for educating students in the vital critical thinking and questioning skills they will need to use throughout their lives.

Teachers who have learned, practiced, and taught Questions for Life often share that it is so ingrained in their minds that they cannot think of teaching without making at least some reference to it. What follows is a sampling of actual lesson plans from different educators teaching at different grade levels across the United States. All the lesson plans can be modified, of course, and hopefully they will stir your imagination and inspire you to develop many of your own lesson plans incorporating Questions for Life.

Share your lesson plans with us on our QFL Web site: **www.plsweb.com/QFL**.

Elementary Grades Lesson (Grades 3 to 5): *The Titanic Lost...and Found*

Overview

The first sample Questions for Life lesson covers an elementary school lesson plan developed by a reading specialist. In this third-grade lesson plan, which extends over several days, students read a book about the sinking of the *Titanic* and its later discovery in the ocean. The lesson could be adapted for fourth- and fifth-grade classrooms by adding information, increasing the difficulty of the questions, and/or posing additional questions for more in-depth discussion.

Purpose

The purpose of the lesson was for students to read, interpret, and critically analyze the information in a book titled *The Titanic Lost...and Found* by Judy Donnelly.[1] Each student had a laminated Questions for Life Cue Words card in the upper right-hand corner of his or her desk. As the teacher posed questions using Questions for Life strategies, students were encouraged to use the cue words she articulated in each question to identify the thinking process she asked for and respond accordingly.

Prior Knowledge

To develop prior knowledge about the *Titanic*—or the "Wonder Ship," as it was called—the reading specialist first showed students cross-sectional pictures of the ship. Discussion began with a focus on first-class accommodations, located on the ship's upper decks and featuring luxuriously furnished rooms, including separate dining areas and music rooms. Then the discussion moved to a consideration of the accommodations and conditions on the lower decks that housed the third-class passengers. Students talked about how it would have been to travel in each of those sections of the ship (Perception).

Students were introduced to the word *titanic,* which derives from the Greek word *titan* (the Titans were giants in Greek mythology, so the word *titanic* means "huge" or "powerful"). Students gave their opinions about why *Titanic* was a good name for the ship (Evaluation). They then developed a mind map showing potential dangers at sea, including those that threatened a large ship like the *Titanic* (Analysis).

Section 1: The Wonder Ship

Prior Knowledge

After students read Section 1 of the book, the teacher posed questions using Questions for Life strategies. Constant referral to the laminated Questions for Life Cue Words card on each of their desks allowed students to become familiar with the cue words that signal the type of thinking required in the different questioning strategies.

Questions for Life Row 1

Note that although the type of thinking is listed after each question throughout this lesson, the teacher did not tell the students what kind of thinking they were to do. The words in parentheses are there for the reader's benefit only.

1. What were the *reasons* the *Titanic* was called "The Wonder Ship"? (Analysis)

Sample response:
"The ship had many new features not found on older ships, including restaurants, a post office, a gym, and a swimming pool. It was like a floating palace."

2. *List* features that made the people on the *Titanic* feel safe. (Analysis)

Sample responses:
- "The ship had two hulls, one inside the other."
- "The lowest part of the *Titanic* had 16 watertight compartments. The captain could pull a switch to close off a compartment if it started to flood."
- "A thick steel door would shut and trap the water."
- "Two, three, or even four compartments could be flooded, and the ship would still float."

Guided Visualization: Perception

To heighten students' perceptions of what traveling on the *Titanic* might have been like, and to help them imagine a sensory experience of the events in the story, the teacher led them through a guided visualization intended to elicit Perception.

Sample Visualization:
"The *Titanic* is ready to sail. Picture it as it pulls away from the dock. Notice the passengers outside on the decks. See their hands waving goodbye and throwing kisses to their friends and families. Hear the excitement of the crowds as they watch the huge ship begin its first voyage."

"How would you have *felt* if you were on the *Titanic?*"

Sample response:
"I would have been very excited to be on such a fancy new ship with so much to do and so many people to meet."

Section 2: Iceberg

Prior Knowledge

To develop prior knowledge about this section of the lesson, the reading specialist and her students talked about what can be done if a ship experiences trouble at sea. The reading specialist led the students to understand that people must rely on the expertise of those running the ship. One little girl said that it was the same as flying on an airplane: passengers must rely on the experience of the captain like they rely on the pilot to help in case of an emergency (Insight).

Questions for Life: Rows 1, 2, and 3

While encouraging students to refer to their Questions for Life Cue Words cards, the reading specialist then asked questions and told the students to identify and recite back to her the type of question asked before responding.

1. What *steps* were taken when the lookout spotted the iceberg? (Analysis)

   Sample response:
   "The question is an Analysis question because the word *steps* is a cue word for Analysis. The lookout became afraid and rang the alarm, crying out: 'Iceberg straight ahead!' The seaman turned the ship, but it was too late. The giant iceberg scraped along the side of the ship, causing damage."

2. What *sequence* of events took place when the captain heard a grinding sound? (Analysis)

   Sample response:
   "That is an Analysis question too. The captain went below to assess the damage and realized the *Titanic* was badly hurt. Five of the watertight compartments were already flooded and nothing else could be done. The captain sent out an order to wake the passengers and radioed messages for help."

3. What *insights* or *realizations* do you have about the passengers, who continued to laugh and listen to music even after the sailors ordered them to get into lifeboats? (Insight)

   Sample response:
   "You used the words *insights* and *realizations,* which call for Insight thinking. My insight is that the passengers were not worried because they felt that the *Titanic* could not sink."

4. What *procedures* did the passengers follow to get into the lifeboats? (Analysis)

   Sample response:
   "*Procedure* is a cue word for an Analysis question. The women and children went first, and the men could get into a lifeboat only if there was room."

5. What *generalizations* can you make about the experiences of the passengers on the lower decks as they tried to get up to the lifeboats? (Induction)

Sample response:
"You want us to use Induction. The passengers on the lower decks had trouble getting out because many of the staircases had already been blocked. They had to wait around because the first-class passengers had better access to help. On the whole, they became very scared."

6. *In a nutshell,* what made communication poor with the neighboring ship, the *Californian?* (Summary)

Sample response:
"*Nutshell* means Summary! Although the *Californian* was less than 20 miles from the *Titanic,* the operator had turned off his radio. The crew of the *Titanic* had to set off rockets to let the sailors on the *Californian* know they were in trouble. The sailors on the *Californian* never realized that the *Titanic* needed help, maybe because they, too, thought the *Titanic* could never sink."

7. *Sequence* the stages of the sinking of the *Titanic* from the time the lower decks were underwater to when it went down (Analysis).

Sample response:
"That's an Analysis question. The lower decks were underwater, two lifeboats were left, and some people were jumping into the icy waters. Some of them reached lifeboats and others remained in the freezing water. Those in lifeboats rowed away from the *Titanic.* One end of the ship slid into the ocean. The other end swung straight up. Then the *Titanic* slid under the icy black water."

8. The musicians playing on deck stopped playing happy music and started playing a hymn. What *insight* do you have about why the music changed? (Insight)

   Sample response:
   "That's an Insight question. Here's my realization: I think a hymn meant that all hope was lost, and the *Titanic* would soon sink."

Section 3: Never Again

Prior Knowledge

Again, the reading specialist referred students to the laminated cards on their desks showing the Questions for Life model that would help to imprint the cue words into their memories. She wanted to ensure that as they heard or read the cue words in the questions, they would naturally and automatically respond with the thinking process triggered by the cue word.

Questions for Life: Rows 1, 2, and 3

1. *Mind map* how the people in the lifeboats survived (Analysis).

   Sample response:
   After noting that they were being asked to use Analysis, students created a mind map, as follows:

   • In a center circle they wrote, "How People Survived."
   • In an oval coming off the center they wrote, "Leaning," for the men who leaned this way and that to help keep the boats from tilting.
   • In another oval off the center they wrote, "Rescue," for the

one lifeboat that went back to save a man who was floating on a wooden door.
- In yet another oval they wrote, "Huddled for warmth."

2. *Summarize* how the ship *Carpathia* rescued the survivors of the *Titanic*.

Sample response:
"I can do Summary! It took many hours to get the people on board. They had to lift them up to the deck one boat at a time. Everyone who climbed aboard was saved."

3. What safety *procedures* changed after the *Titanic* disaster to make ships safer? (Analysis)

Sample response:
"That's an Analysis question. There were only enough lifeboats for 1,178 of the 2,227 passengers on the *Titanic,* so procedures changed to require ships to have enough lifeboats to accommodate every single passenger. Ship radios had to stay on during the entire voyage. Every ship had to have a lifeboat drill so people would know what to do if there was an accident."

4. What *changes* would you make to this list of procedures to make sure no other ships could sink at sea? (Idea)

Sample responses:
- "Here are my ideas. I would make everyone wear a lifejacket all the time, even when they were dancing."
- "I would put more lifeboats on the ship so more people could get into them."

- "People in lower decks would be able to get out from the bottom into boats, and people from the upper decks could get out by climbing into a helicopter."

Multiple Intelligences Centers: Action

After the class finished reading the story, the teacher assigned students to centers that matched Howard Gardner's multiple intelligences. In these centers the students participated in the Action part of the Questions for Life model, as described below. The teacher used Action cue words, such as *create, draw, write, role-play, construct.* In most cases the Action was requested through a statement rather than through a question.

Center #1: Bodily Kinesthetic/Musical/Rhythmic Intelligences

Prior Knowledge

The group at this center reviewed the fact that the radio aboard the *Titanic* was a wireless telegraph, a machine used to tap out and receive messages in Morse code (letters were replaced by "dots" and "dashes"). The students received a copy of the Morse code and were given time to learn which dot and dash symbols represented which letters.

The Action Statement

The reading specialist gave the following statement requiring students to respond with Action: "Practice Morse code (used by the *Titanic* radio operators), then make up your own messages, and finally decode one another's messages."

Sample responses:
- A student demonstrated an SOS call: three taps, three dashes, and three taps.
- Students practiced with Morse code to write their own SOS messages.
- Students exchanged papers and decoded one another's messages.

Center #2: Bodily Kinesthetic

Prior Knowledge

Having learned that the word *nautical* refers to water and ships, the students were given a list of nautical terms.

The Action Statement

Students responded to the following Action statement: "*Create* and *act* out a nautical game using symbols that represent nautical terms."

Sample response:
Students developed a game by creating motions to symbolize the nautical terms. For example, they created hand movements to represent hoisting *the sails*, *bailing*, and the locations of the *port* and *leeward* sides of a ship.

Center #3: Interpersonal Intelligence

Prior Knowledge

Students were told to work together to review the graphic in their text showing the cross sections of the *Titanic* and its various compartments. Students worked in pairs researching other views of the *Titanic* on the Internet.

The Action Statement

Students responded to the following Action statement: "Work in pairs to examine and discuss the various sections of the *Titanic* diagrams. Then pairs will come together to reach consensus on developing a *drawing* of the whole ship (or part(s) of it); label each area (for example, stateroom, restaurant, engine room, swimming pool)."

Sample response:
The pairs decided together to diagram the lower parts of the ship where the engines were located, where the iceberg hit, and where the water first flowed in; they labeled each of these sections appropriately.

Center #4: Intrapersonal Intelligence

Prior Knowledge

Working individually, students skimmed the boldface headings of the story.

The Action Statement

"Working quietly and individually, *write* open-ended entries in your journals about your own thoughts on taking a voyage that ended with such hardship."

Sample response:
One student wrote in his journal about the time he fell

down when he was pretending to be a "titan," and how those who bragged about the *Titanic* probably felt very bad after it sank.

Center #5: Naturalist Intelligence

Prior Knowledge

Before the work in centers began, students made replicas of icebergs by freezing water in containers of various sizes.

The Action Statement

"Using the ice you froze in containers, *sketch* a side view of what a floating iceberg might look like as it melts. *Analyze* and chart your results."

> Sample response:
> Students measured each of their icebergs. They then put the icebergs into a pan of water and quickly sketched them as they began to melt. Then they removed them and measured them again. They repeated the procedure several times, writing down the changing measurements next to their drawings.

Section 4: Found at Last

Prior Knowledge

Students silently read the final part of the book, "Found at Last." The following Questions for Life were asked when they finished.

Questions for Life: Rows 1, 2, and 3

1. Robert Ballard had dreamed of finding the *Titanic* ever since he was a little boy. He pictured what it would look like and talked about it often. What *qualities* did his focus on the *Titanic* demonstrate about Robert Ballard? (Induction)

    Sample response:
    "*Qualities* means you're asking an Induction question. From his focus on the *Titanic*, I would say Robert Ballard's qualities were dedication and perseverance, because he was a scientist who continued to follow his dream. He was probably was really excited to finally discover the *Titanic*."

2. *List* what Argo, the robot, could do underwater. (Analysis)

    Sample responses:
    *   "You gave an Analysis statement. Argo could dive down very deep."
    *   "The robot could take underwater video pictures."
    *   "The pictures Argo took were sent to a TV screen on the ship."

3. What did Robert and the other scientists *see* when they found the *Titanic* on the ocean floor? (Perception)

    Sample response:
    "You are asking us a Perception question. The *Titanic* had broken apart, so they saw its pieces. Robert saw the crow's nest, where the lookout had first seen the iceberg. The giant anchors were there. Glass windows lay in the sand. There were bottles of wine, dishes, and suitcases on the ocean floor."

4. Of all the messages Robert Ballard left behind, what was the *most* important? (Appraisal)

   Sample response:
   "You are asking for Appraisal. The most important message Robert Ballard left was that he wanted the great ship to be left in peace."

5. *Predict* how the survivors might have reacted if they had been alive to learn about the discovery of the *Titanic* (Prediction).

   Sample responses:
   • "I need to do a prediction. I would predict that those who lost members of their families would have been very sad to be reminded of the tragedy."
   • "I believe there were some who would have still remembered how beautiful the *Titanic* was."

Culminating Activity

The reading specialist then asked her students to form groups and create five questions of their own based on the story. They were asked to use the Questions for Life cue words in each question. When they were finished, students joined another group and played a game in which they asked the other group their questions.

Middle School Lesson (Grades 6 to 8): Brown v. Board of Education

Overview

This middle school lesson plan, Brown v. Board of Education, was used with students who had already learned and used the Questions for Life model in this classroom and others. The lesson plan assumes a certain amount of preparation given by the teacher, who had delivered brief lectures and provided background information about discrimination against African Americans in the United States. The teacher brought to life the important historical events that had led up to the Supreme Court decision on May 17, 1954.

Their understanding of these events set up the lesson for students who read the story "Brown vs. Board of Education" by Walter Dean Myers in the anthology *Out of Tune*.[2] The teacher used Questions for Life questioning strategies to guide students' thinking about the content of the reading.

Purpose

The purpose of having middle school students read the story "Brown vs. Board of Education" by Walter Dean Myers was to help them understand the experience of African Americans who were discriminated against and deprived of the rights and privileges afforded others in the United States.

Using the cue words from the Questions for Life model, the teacher formulated and asked questions following a silent reading of the text.

Prior Knowledge

Before students read Myers' story about the Brown v. Board of Education decision, the teacher introduced and led a discussion on how the Supreme Court is empowered to interpret the United States Constitution and determine the constitutionality of laws passed by Congress and state legislatures.

Teacher and students also researched and discussed the Fourteenth Amendment, which states that all American citizens have equal rights under the law. The teacher related the story of

Thurgood Marshall, an African American, who became an influential attorney and then sat as a Supreme Court Justice from 1967 to 1991. As a young boy, Marshall, the great-grandson of a slave, read the words of the Fourteenth Amendment and wondered how segregation could exist when the Constitution promised everyone equal rights.

Students learned that in many parts of the United States African Americans had once been referred to as "coloreds." Historical photographs showed that they were not allowed to eat at the same restaurants as white people and that they were forced to sit at the backs of buses, use separate restrooms, and drink from water fountains marked *colored*. They were often deprived of the right to vote.

Questions for Life: Analysis

"*Define* what freedom meant to the Africans who were captured and brought to the United States in slave ships with their wrists chained." (Analysis)

"*Define* the meaning of *freedom* as it had changed for African Americans by the 1900s." (Analysis)

"The ruling of the Supreme Court in the 1896 Plessy v. Ferguson case stated that it was legal to have facilities that were 'separate but equal.' *Analyze* the effect this Supreme Court ruling had on African Americans." (Analysis)

Questions for Life: Perception

A short visualization using Perception followed the Analysis questions so students could better understand the meaning of segregation:

Linda Brown, a third-grade African-American student, was told she could not attend her neighborhood public school in Topeka, Kansas. *See* the disappointed look on her face as she walks a mile through a railroad switchyard to get to the bus stop for the ride to the Monroe school where all the children are Black. *Notice* how dilapidated the school is. *Observe* the broken ceiling tiles, crumbling floors, unplastered walls, and smashed windows.

"How would you *feel* about having to attend a different school from the one other children attend because of the color of your skin?"

Questions for Life: Induction

"What *generalization* might Linda Brown make as she *sees* that she is separated from white children in the neighborhood and *observes* the condition of her school compared to that of the white children's school only a few blocks away?"

Questions for Life: Insight

"Let's pretend that a law is passed that would prohibit any male or female with brown eyes from entering a football stadium. What *insights* do you have concerning this law?"

Questions for Life: Analysis

"*List* what values Thurgood Marshall and his family considered important in life."

"Cite *reasons* why Thurgood Marshall and the National Association for the Advancement of Colored People (NAACP) wanted segregation to end in education."

Questions for Life: Evaluation and Analysis

"In your *opinion,* was Thurgood Marshall a good choice to head the legal team that argued that segregation was a violation of the Fourteenth Amendment in Brown v. Board of Education? Cite *reasons* for your answer."

Questions for Life: Summary

"*Summarize* how Kenneth Clark's study of African-American children helped to prove the harmful effects of segregation."

Questions for Life: Appraisal

"List and *prioritize* in order of importance three reasons why Brown v. Board of Education is one of the most important cases ever to come before the Supreme Court."

Questions for Life: Prediction

"*Predict* how your life and the lives of other students would be different if the Supreme Court had not ruled against segregation in 1954."

Questions for Life: Action Activities

As a follow-up activity, students were asked to select and complete one of the activities listed below. Each is based on Questions for Life Action questioning strategies.

Giving students an Action activity in the classroom empowered them to transfer the Questions for Life thinking skills to real life. Guided by their progression through the Questions for Life thinking strategies, students were more comfortable taking Action because they had a deeper knowledge of the events described in the reading and the lesson.

Prior to beginning work on their Action activities the students were asked to list the Questions for Life thinking processes they would need to use in order to complete the assignment successfully. This served as a plan to set up the Action activity and became a useful tool for the thinking involved in planning and developing their work.

> "If you were Thurgood Marshall, what would you say in presenting your case to the Court? *Draft* a response as though you were speaking to the Justices."

> "Research and *write* about the life of Linda Brown after the Brown v. Board of Education ruling. Did she continue to be involved in the Civil Rights Movement?"

> "Research the important dates in the life of Thurgood Marshall and *construct* a timeline."

> "*Write* a brief magazine article about the life of Thurgood Marshall. Include his greatest accomplishment and the qualities he possessed that helped him to overcome the various challenges he faced."

High School or Advanced Middle School Math Lesson: Solving a Word Problem

Word Problem: A can containing 40 marbles weighs 160 grams. The same can is emptied and refilled with 30 marbles and now weighs 132 grams. How much does the empty can weigh?

Solving the Problem Using Questions for Life

- Read the problem and *notice* all its parts (Perception).

- *Visualize* the problem in your mind (Perception).

- *Sort* out the important information that is given (Analysis).

- *Sum up* what the problem is asking for in your own words (Summary).

- *List* the givens (important information) in a table or chart (Analysis).

- *Compare* (check) the numbers you recorded with those in the problem (Same/Different).

Possible Table

First Can Fill	Second Can Fill
20 Marbles	15 Marbles
80 Grams	66 Grams

- How is the first can fill *different* from the second can fill? (Same/Different)

- *List* (record) those differences on your chart (Analysis).

First Fill	Second Fill	Differences
20 Marbles	15 Marbles	5 Marbles
80 Grams	66 Grams	14 Grams

- What *generalizations* can you draw from your chart? (Induction)

- What are some *ways* in which your chart and your generalizations can help you solve the problem? (Idea)

- *Weigh* and then decide which way might be the *best* approach for solving the problem. (Appraisal)

  (Many would suggest finding 1 marble weight and multiplying by 20 or 15. Others would suggest multiplying the 10 marble weight by 4 and by 3.)

- Test *(compute)* your choice. (Action)

1 Marble Weight	Process for 30 Marbles	Process for 40 Marbles
1 Marble		
2.8 Grams	2.8 x 20 = 56 Grams	2.8 x 15 = 42 Grams

Or

5 Marble Weight	Process for 30 Marbles	Process for 40 Marbles
5 Marbles		
14 Grams	14 x 4 = 56 Grams	14 x 3 = 42 Grams

- Check (*compare*) the chart's accuracy. (Same/Different)

- *Compare* the two action steps. (Same/Different)

- Which is the *best* of the two ways? (Appraisal)

- Now that we know the weight of both 30 and 40 marbles, what is the next *step* of the problem? (Analysis)

First Can Fill	Second Can Fill
20 Marbles + Can	15 Marbles + Can
80 Grams	66 Grams
20 marbles	15 Marbles
56 Grams	42 Grams

- *List* the data pieces in the table that are necessary for a solution. (Analysis)

  (The answer appears in gray above in column one (80/56) and in gray in column two (66/42). Either way shows the can weighs 24 grams.)

- *Predict* how organizing the table differently might help in the final solution. (Prediction)

- *Redo* the table to better represent the data. (Action)

	Marbles + Can Weight	Marbles Weight	Can Weight
First Can Fill 20 Marbles	80 Grams	56 Grams	24 Grams
Second Can Fill 15 Marbles	66 Grams	42 Grams	24 Grams

High School Lesson: Product Design

Overview

This lesson was included in a high school course on Interpersonal Communications within a unit on Consensus Decision Making.

Students Choose and Analyze an Advertisement

Students *sorted* through a variety of magazines and chose the advertisement that *most* grabbed their attention (Appraisal). Then they reflected and answered the following Perception questions before they formed and worked in groups.

- What elements did you *notice* first in the advertisement—what caught your attention?
- What did you *see* in the advertisement after you examined it more carefully?
- What *feelings* did the advertisement invoke in you?

In groups students shared their chosen advertisements and their perceptions about the advertisements as they used the following Questions for Life thinking skills:

- Students *compared* and *contrasted* their chosen advertisements (Same/Different).
- Students made a *list* of various elements in their advertisements (Analysis).
- Students made *generalizations* about the *common elements* of effective advertisements (Induction).

Students Create a New Product

Each group was then asked to *create* an imaginary product for its contemporaries from a nontoxic, low-cost gel, and *design* an advertisement to market the product. (Action) Students responded to the following questions and statements from Questions for Life:

- Brainstorm *options* for potential product ideas (Idea). (Each group generated at least 10 to 15 potential ideas.)

- Make *connections* to students your age (Insight).

- *Prioritize* the list in order to focus your attention on the *best* ideas (Appraisal).

- *Predict* the appeal of your ideas (Prediction).

- *Compare* and *contrast* the various ideas (Same/Different).

- Share *opinions* regarding the various ideas (Evaluation).

- *Weigh* ideas, then select what the group feels is its *best* idea (Appraisal).

Students Design the New Product

- Brainstorm *ideas* for potential features of the product (Idea).
- Make *connections* to students in your age group (Insight).
- *List* components you want in the new product (Analysis).
- *Predict* the outcome of using the various design components (Prediction).
- *Compare* and *contrast* the various ideas (Same/Different).
- Share *opinions* regarding the various ideas (Evaluation).
- Select the *best* elements for the new product (Appraisal).
- *Design* the new product (Action).

Students Design an Advertisement for the New Product

- Brainstorm *ideas* for potential elements of an advertisement of the new product (Idea).
- Make *connections* to your age group and to other advertisements studied (Insight).
- *List* components you want in the advertisement (Analysis).

- *Predict* the outcome of using the various advertising components (Prediction).
- *Compare* and *contrast* the advertisement ideas (Same/Different).
- Share *opinions* regarding the various ideas (Evaluation).
- Select the *best* elements for the advertisement (Appraisal).
- *Design* the advertisement (Action).

In the brainstorming sessions the teacher looked for a large number of potential ideas and then looked at the group's ability to analyze information and refine their choices to the best one. As you may have noticed, the Questions for Life process was repeated several times as students:

1. Selected an idea.
2. Designed the product.
3. Designed the advertisement.

Each time students went through the process, they practiced well-thought-out, informed decision making. Students experienced the reality of less creative, less innovative, and less effective choices when shortcuts were taken and the process was not developed in its entirety.

References

Listed in order of appearance

Introduction

1. National Center on Education and the Economy (2006). *Tough choices or tough times: The report on the new commission on the skills of the American workforce.* San Francisco: Jossey-Bass. (© 2007, National Center on Education and economy, p, xxi)

Chapter 1

1. Christensen, C. M., Johnson, C. W., & Horn, M. B. (2008). *Disrupting class: How disruptive innovation will change the way the world learns.* New York: McGraw Hill.

2. Taleb, N. N. (2007). *The black swan: The impact of the highly improbable.* New York: Random House. Used by permission of Random House, Inc.

3. Partnership for 21st Century Skills (2008). 21st *century skills, education & competitiveness: A resource and policy guide.* Tucson, AZ: Partnership for 21st Century Skills. (www.21stcenturyskills. org) The Partnership for 21st Century Skills is the leading advocacy organization focused on infusing 21st century skills into education.

4. Pink, D. H. (2006). *A whole new mind: Why right-brainers will rule the future.* New York: Riverhead Trade.

Chapter 3

1. The Bill and Melinda Gates Foundation. The 3R's Solution. (www.gatesfoundation.org)

2. The Metro High School, created by Ohio State University and The Education Council of Columbus, Ohio, emphasizes science, technology, engineering, and math (also referred to as STEM). (www.themetroschool.com)

3. Battelle: A scientific research think tank. (www.battelle.org)

4. Chicago's Public School's Student Zone, an example of project-based learning.

5. Strategic National Education Plan from the Ministry of Education in Aruba. General Board of Higher Education and Ministry.

6. Partnership for 21st Century Skills. (www.21stcenturyskills.org)

7. Grantham, C., Ware, J. P., & Williamson, C. (2007). *Corporate agility: A revolutionary new model for competing in a flat world.* Saranac, NY: AMACOM Books. The Future of Work (www.thefutureofwork.net)

8. From an interview by Terri Bianco of Jim Ware on October 27, 2008. James P. Ware and Charles Grantham, Work Design Collaborative, LLC., Berkeley, CA. (www.thefutureofwork.net)

Chapter 4

1. Anderson, L. W., & Krathwohl, D. R. (Eds.). (2001). *A taxonomy for learning, teaching, and assessing: A revision of Bloom's Taxonomy of Educational Objectives.* New York: Addison Wesley Longman.

2. Card Game Rules. www.pagat.com/vying/pokerrules.html. www.pagat.com/rummy/ginrummy.html

3. Wolk, S. (2008). School as inquiry. *Phi Delta Kappan, 90*(2), 115-122.

Chapter 5

1. Douglas, E. F. (1998). *Straight talk: Turning communication upside down for strategic results at work.* Palo Alto, CA: Davies-Black. Used with permission.

2. Hall, P., & Simeral, A. (2008). *Building teachers' capacity for success: A collaborative approach for coaches and school leaders.* Alexandria, VA: Association for Supervision and Curriculum Development. (p. 9) Reprinted by permission. Learn more aboout ASCD at www.ascd.org

Chapter 6

1. The Community Partnership for Mindfulness in Education, Park Day School, Oakland, CA. K-8, Classrooms adding M for meditation. (2009, February 9). The *Sacramento Bee,* p. A1. (www.parkdayschool.org.)

Chapter 8

1. Douglas, E. F. (1998). *Straight talk: Turning communication upside down for strategic results at work.* Palo Alto, CA: Davies-Black (Circle of Assumptions: p. 102.)

2. Collins, J. (2001). *Good to great: Why some companies make the leap...and others don't.* San Francisco, CA: Collins Business. (References to Stockdale reprinted with permission of Jim Collins.)

3. Stockdale, J., and Stockdale, S. (1990). *In love and war: The story of a family's ordeal and sacrifice during the Vietnam years.* Annapolis, MD: Naval Institute Press.

4. McGinnis, A. L. (1994). The *power of optimism.* New York: Random House Value Publishing.

5. Haggart, W. (1995). *The Kaleidoscope Profile.* Nevada City, CA: Performance Learning Systems, Inc. (www.plsweb.com)

6. Myers, I. B., & Briggs, K. (1950). *Myers-Briggs temperament types.* Gainesville, FL: The Myers-Briggs Foundation. (www.myersbriggs.org)

7. Voice Dialogue. (www.voicedialogue.com)

8. Frank, A. (1989). *Diary of Anne Frank.* New York: Longman Books.

Chapter 9

1. Simpson-West, D., & Yeates, J. (2008). *Behavioral, academic, and social interventions for the classroom.* [Graduate course]. Cadiz, KY: Performance Learning Systems, Inc. (www.plsweb.com.)

Appendix

1. J. Donnelly, (1999). *The Titanic Lost...and Found.* St Louis, MO: San Val.

2. Myers, W. D. (1995). Brown vs. board of education. In the anthology reader *Out of tune.* Lexington, MA/Toronto, Canada: D.C. Heath and Company.

Using Materials From This Book

Reproducing the Questions for Life Cue Words card or any of the Figures in this book is encouraged if you are supporting a group that is learning about Questions for Life. We want you to be able to use this book to become as effective as possible at using the Questions for Life skills. Therefore, as an educator teaching classroom students or a group of other educators, you are free to reproduce and distribute the card and any figure(s) that are helpful to the students or educators you are teaching. Note: You cannot reproduce text, which is copyrighted—only Figures and the card.

However, reproducing Figures and the Questions for Life Cue Words card from this book to conduct fee-for-service training requires Performance Learning Systems' written permission. If a group has retained you specifically to train them in Questions for Life, you may not reproduce *any* pages without express written permission from Performance Learning Systems, Inc. Our policies are fair and supportive, and we ask that you make a reasonable contribution if you are benefiting financially from our work. To gain permission for these purposes, please contact Beth Eck at Performance Learning Systems, Permissions Department, 800-343-4484.

We highly recommend that teachers who instruct other educators in Questions for Life practice using the skills themselves and require educators to read *Questions for Life: Powerful Strategies to Guide Critical Thinking.*

We provide **group discounts on books**. Contact Jackie Futrell, PLS Products, at 800-506-9996 for details on group discounts.

Index

Note
- Page numbers followed by *fig* indicate figures.
- Page numbers followed by *+fig* indicate discussions plus figures.
- Page numbers followed by *qtn* indicate quotations.
- Page numbers followed by *+qtn* indicate discussions plus quotations.
- Page ranges "hyphenated" by "/", as in "10/12",
indicate discussions interrupted by full-page figures.

About the Author

Stephen G. Barkley serves as Executive Vice President of Performance Learning System, Inc. He has 32 years' experience teaching educators and administrators in school districts, state departments, teacher organizations, and institutions of higher education throughout the United States and internationally. A riveting motivational keynote speaker, trainer, consultant, and facilitator, Steve is known for increasing clients' effort and success by sharing his knowledge and experience. His questioning skill is key to his facilitation success.

You may contact Steve at:

6227 Lower Mountain Road
New Hope, PA 18938
888-424-9700
Fax: 215-862-4884
sbarkley@plsweb.com

Steve's earlier books, *Quality Teaching in a Culture of Coaching, Wow! Adding Pizzazz to Teaching and Learning,* and *Tapping Student Effort~Increasing Student Achievement* have contributed to teacher and student learning and achievement. You may purchase Steve's books, including this one, through:

Performance Learning Systems
72 Lone Oak Drive, Cadiz, KY 42211
800-556-9996
http://www.plsweb.com/resources/products/books

Enhancing Teaching and Learning

When choosing professional development for your school, it is important to consider a source that is effective and proven to be successful. Performance Learning System's professional development enhances teaching and learning and we practice what we teach.

PLS Guaranteed Professional Development Service Offer

All levels of school involvement including teachers, administrators, coaches, para-professionals, parents, and school-board members can benefit from the teaching PLS consistently delivers. PLS instructors work with your staff to find positive solutions for your specific challenges.

- Interactive Workshops
- Online Professional Development
- In-Service Trainings
- Government-mandated Program

Excellent Reputation for Effective Delivery

PLS has established working relationships with regional, national, and international educational organizations. Many successful major educational initiatives throughout the U.S. have also been supported by PLS.

With professional learning communities teachers continually learn and are focused on student needs. This will provide a framework for consistent, intensive messages that professional development is important in achieving student performance. It's a collective responsibility. Steve Barkley has made an enormous impact on this program with NJ educators. He creates a sense of urgency.
—Vicki Duff, Teacher Quality Control Coordinator
NJ Department of Education

To learn more about professional development and consulting opportunities, visit us at www.plsweb.com/PD1109. Or call us today at 888-424-9700 to schedule a workshop or training.

PERFORMANCE
LEARNING SYSTEMS

More Books by Steve Barkley

Steve's books have contributed to teacher and student learning and increased achievement.

Quality Teaching in a Culture of Coaching

Incorporate a culture of coaching into your own educational environment.

WOW!
Adding Pizzazz to Teaching and Learning

Learn how to make school experiences so outstanding that students, parents, and colleagues will say "WOW!"

Tapping Student Effort
Increasing Student Achievement

Discover ways to generate enthusiasm and motivation in students so they want to exert effort.

You may purchase Steve's books at:
Performance Learning Systems
72 Lone Oak Drive, Cadiz, KY 42211
800-556-9996
www.plsweb.com/resources

PERFORMANCE
LEARNING SYSTEMS

Schedule Steve Barkley
to Speak at Your Next
Professional Development Event!

Steve's keynotes are skill-based with concrete examples and insightful stories, and can be effectively followed by smaller group workshops conducted by Steve and/or additional PLS staff.

Topics and titles include:

- The Magic of Excellent Teaching
- Power of Optimism
- Teambuilding
- Raising Student Expectations
- Discovering the Power of Live-Event Learning
- Peer Coaching
- Facilitation Skills for Leaders
- Leadership for Innovation and Change
- Facilitating Professional Learning Communities
- Principal/Coach Partnerships

For more information, or to schedule
a keynote or professional development day in your district,
call Steve Barley or Barry Zvolenski at 888-424-9700.

PERFORMANCE
LEARNING SYSTEMS

Notes

Notes

CPSIA information can be obtained
at www.ICGtesting.com
Printed in the USA
BVOW04s0434091117
499855BV00010B/343/P